Unearthed

Digging the Jewels of Sobriety
from the Trenches of Addiction

PATRICIA MONASMITH

iUniverse, Inc.
Bloomington

Unearthed
Digging the Jewels of Sobriety from the Trenches of Addiction

iUniverse books may be ordered through booksellers or by contacting:

iUniverse
1663 Liberty Drive
Bloomington, IN 47403
www.iuniverse.com
1-800-Authors (1-800-288-4677)

ISBN: 978-1-4502-8308-3 (pbk)
ISBN: 978-1-4502-8311-3 (ebk)

Printed in the United States of America

iUniverse rev. date: 1/10/2011

Contents

Acknowledgments

I would like to thank God for giving me the creativity to do what I do. To my children: Jason, Bryan and Amber, I would like to say, you are my inspiration. Bob, Peggy and Karri, you guys rock! Thanks for all of your help. I couldn't have done this without you. To my siblings Jack, Glenda, and Tracy, I can't begin to thank you for all you have done and for all the times you bailed me out, I won't forget. To my Dad, I love you so much, thanks for always being there for me.

Thank you all.

Introduction

I taught as a Counselor's Assistant for a drug and alcohol facility. My work consisted of trying to transform beat up, wounded, frustrated, hopeless human beings, into healthy, productive citizens that could live in mainstream society.

When clients walked through the door of our facility I would try to sift through the confusion of their lives to find the gold nuggets and diamond like characteristics that I know are deep with-in the make-up of this special population.

Much like these individuals are my writings. What you will find with-in the pages of this book will be imperfection. I am a recovering addict and the way I write is rough around the edges and sometimes hard to follow. I believe my work reflects my character. I really like it that way. My hope is that you will take this opportunity and sift this piece like you would if you were panning for gold or digging for diamonds. Somewhere in the midst of it all are precious morsels of my life. Although what you read won't be perfect, I hope it will at least be interesting.

While writing this book I'm in the process of changing careers. Part of this book has been written while at my current job. I'm transitioning into the ministry as I write. I hope to be ministering full time before this book is finished.

Dressed for Battle

THE DAY HAD FINALLY ARRIVED and I was very nervous. It would be the first time that I would speak as a full-time minister of the Lord. It wasn't in a traditional setting. I knew it wouldn't be. I wasn't preaching, I was presenting and sowing the word of God as He was showing it to me.

I love to present the word through visuals so that everyone can get a complete understanding of the word. I had my sister Glenda assist me. She has always been gracious to help me with those kinds of things. She stood there as I began by sharing my testimony of where God was taking me. When it was time she gladly called out; "ready to report for duty sir." I was to portray the Commander in Chief, though I could never fill those shoes, I knew my audience would get the message. I began by sharing how when you get saved you must sign in as a soldier of the Lord. It is simple, all it takes is a willing heart to accept what the Lord has done, and ask Him into your heart. The soldier was more than willing to oblige.

The next step was to dress for battle. I would never want anyone to go onto the field of battle without proper attire. I told those listening of a vision I had of me on a mine field crawling on my stomach, fully dressed in battle gear. I had other soldiers on my right side and they too were on their stomachs crawling very slowly across the field. We knew that the field was full of mines and our mission was to disarm the mines that would explode, if touched. It was frustrating because we couldn't tell where the mines were, and that made it difficult to complete our mission.

All of a sudden, a great wind blew from behind us, and when it did, it blew all the sand off the mines and we were able to see where each mine laid. We were able to disarm each one without injury. This made it safe for the others we knew were coming behind us. We were aware that this was the wind of the Holy Spirit and that the mines were put there by the devil to kill us.

1

Our mission was successful, thanks to the Holy Spirit. I knew when I had this vision that there would be a day coming when I would teach on spiritual warfare and this night started the journey.

I picked up a belt and began to put it around my soldier. I explained how the belt of a soldier held tight to all the other pieces of armor and how important it was for the soldier to know that the belt represented truth. If we don't walk in truth, we lose the battle.

I then picked up the breastplate. It represented the breastplate of righteousness. I explained to the soldier that this piece was a very important piece of armor and without it, we will never gain access into the gates of Heaven. This piece was the piece that represented the blood of Jesus and it was the only thing that the Father sees when He looks at us. When Jesus took His blood and applied it to the mercy seat in Heaven, it granted us entrance to the Holy of Holies. It doesn't matter if we win the battles, we know that there are times when we will lose, but with the breastplate, we have already won the war.

I then took the helmet of salvation and placed it on the soldier's head. I felt so warm inside as I did this. This piece was so special for me. It represented Jesus' life. It was the ransom paid for me, His life for mine. Once this helmet was on, I never had to worry about taking it off. It was an awesome gift the Father had given.

I then brought out a pair of combat boots. These represented the feet shod with the preparation of piece each Christian must walk in. When you walk in the peace of the gospel, you know that every step you take is ordered of the Lord. "Always keep your boots of peace on" I said to the soldier.

She was fully dressed for battle but I wasn't finished yet. I then brought out a shield, representing the shield of faith that quenches every fiery dart of the enemy. This shield is able to have each dart that the enemy fires, and as it penetrates into the shield, quenched. One must understand that the battle we fight against the enemy is most of the time fought in our mind. I read once that Jesus was crucified at Golgotha, translated, "The place of the Skull" because we fight our battles in the mind, how fitting. This is done, by "bringing every thought we think, captive." (2 Cor. 10:5).

No soldier is complete without having a sword. I brought out a sword and explained how the word of God is the sword that is sharp and able to divide the spirit from the soul. We should always use this sword with the shield of faith. They work beautifully together.

Ephesians 6:12 covers all this material. It talks about the armor. The Lord had showed me through Eph. 6 what actually made the armor what it was. My soldier was fully prepared for battle. I then told the soldier that the post she would be assigned to was the post of responsibility and that the battle would be fought on her knees. All our spiritual battles are. We don't actually fight the battles, the Lord says that "the victory is ours when the battles the Lords". (1 Cor. 15:57). This was so exciting that I could hardly speak. To think that the Lord fights our battle's for us and we are the ones that see the victory. Not only do we get to have the victory, we also get to collect the booty. When king Jehoshaphat was facing a battle where 3 mighty nations were coming against him, the Lord gave him instruction on what to do. He prayed and fasted and showed up for the battle but the Lord fought for Him and when it was all over, the king's people spent 3 days collecting the booty. Now that's what I call more than conquers. (2 Chronicles 20). I will be talking about this later, in another part of the book.

I didn't realize it until later, but it was brought to my attention, that there were four men walking back and forth passed our door all evening as we were presenting this information to our listeners. Before the night had actually began, the Lord had given me the gift of Discernment and I was able to see some things in the spirit that concerned me about the place we were presenting the spiritual warfare boot camp. I understood the compromising position we could have been put in if the Lord hadn't been protecting us. I looked out across the parking lot and it was completely empty. This was a weekend night and the parking lot should have been filled. I decided after that, to only have these meetings in the churches we would be visiting so that we would have the home court advantage.

We began to pray and there was a word of prophecy that came forth, and then the meeting was brought to a close. As everyone left, I noticed my partner was sensing something very strange, I ask her what was going on and she said, "oh nothing", I knew that I was seeing something so I pushed her to tell me what was going on. She then began to explain to me that she had saw legs running toward her. They were dark and they were swift. She said she thought it might have been her hair that she saw. It was a little too descriptive to be her hair and I know it had meaning. We're not sure why she saw it, but I know it is significant. Time will tell, but for now, we'll just have to wait.

The Lord blessed us that night. It was the first fruits of many interesting nights to come.

The Harvest

THERE HAS NEVER BEEN A harvest without planting a seed. When I think about seeds, I think about the seeds that produce food. In fact, there are all kinds of things that you can plant. My mind has been so closed, until just recently; I never gave sowing and planting very much thought.

All my Christian life I have planted seeds. I've planted seeds of the Lord from His word, seeds of money that was given because I'm a tither, Seeds of encouragement when others needed a pick me up. I've always received a great harvest from everything I have ever planted.

Last week the Lord blessed me to know about a harvest that blew my mind when I saw the revelation of it. I was reading in scripture about when someone goes to the altar, if someone has something against you, that you should go to them and fix it and then go back to the altar and take care of business. I was getting ready to speak at a woman's meeting and the message was on sowing and reaping. You might wonder why I was reading a scripture on going to the altar if I was teaching a lesson on sowing.

The Lord works in mysterious ways and I'm so glad he does. As I read Matthew 5:23 I saw something for the first time that made me see the greatest harvest there ever was or will ever be. It says; "Therefore if you bring your gift to the altar, and there remember that your brother has something against you, leave your gift there before the altar, and go your way, first being reconciled to your brother, and then come and offer your gift." I know you can't see it because it's not real obvious, but it's there. I became very curious of the gift that we are to bring to the altar when we come. Was it me, was I the gift? Was I supposed to bring something all these years and haven't brought it? I didn't know.

The Lord led me to The 9th Chapter of Leviticus. The whole chapter talks about the priest bringing their offerings to God when they came. Not just the priest, but the children of Israel. They always brought an offering. If they showed up empty handed or if they brought the wrong thing, (I also had read where the priest's sons offered strange fire before the Lord and died for it. Lev. Chapter 10). The Lord would not receive it.

My mind all of a sudden realized when I read it, that what we bring to the altar, whenever we come, is the blood of Jesus Christ that was shed on our behalf. We carry Jesus in our hearts and it is His blood that was shed at Calvary that God accepts when we come to Him. It's all He sees. Jesus took His blood and applied it to the mercy seat in Heaven when He ascended into Heaven, causing us to be able to have a relationship with the Father, we now can go into the Holy of Holies because of Jesus' blood.

The children of Israel could only offer the blood of bulls and goats, but we can offer the Blood of the Lamb that was slain from the foundation of the world. So, what does that have to do with planting and sowing? God planted His Son in the ground when He died, one seed for all mankind. That seed produced a harvest of blood that covers all who ask Jesus into their hearts. Every time one of God's children goes to the altar, God sees the seed. God experiences a view of the harvest of that incorruptible seed. Millions of people grace the altar of God on a weekly basis, bringing an offering, they don't ever realize that they bring. It is the offering that God accepts so He can have relationship with us who have Jesus in our hearts. It's what allows us into the Holy of Holies. One seed equals a sea of people that can stand before Him because of His Son. Do you see it? What a harvest!

The women I spoke to that night were floored to know that each time they go before the Lord they take a gift. It just makes sense. We should never come before the Lord empty handed. What is so beautiful, is that the Lord not only provided the gift, but it was the very best gift that can ever be given. God only gives the best and He should only receive the best from us and in order for that to happen, Jesus had to be it!

Gone in a Breath

"Tender trees in a tiny meadow, that have shed their golden leaves, waiting for a layer of glistening frost to spread itself against their bare branches, winter has finally arrived."

For as long as I can remember I've wanted to be a writer. Many times I have written things down, hoping that someday those writings would end up in a book, imagine that. That little poem was just a thought that lingered in my mind for a minute. "In a blink of an eye," I had written something I think is so beautiful. It tells a story. I can almost feel a shiver when I think about it.

Many things have happen suddenly in my life, my mother's death is one of them. She was gone before I got a chance to know her. She was murdered by my step-father. It was a murder-suicide. They died like they lived, and when it was all over, they had nothing to show for their lives.

I remember when the call came in. I was living in Texas. I was only 22 and already I was a mother of three beautiful children. Mom had come for a visit a few weeks before she died. I introduced her to the newest addition to our family. My daughter Amber was born in May of 1982 and by August of that year my mother was murdered. Three short months and she only got to see her once. Mom would be proud of the way my daughter turned out.

My Mother loved my children. The two older boys called her their bubble gum grandma. She used to send Jason and Bryan bubble gum through the mail. They were 3 and 5 when we got the news. Before we moved away, she would drive them around, allowing them to stand up beside her, as they traveled slowly down old, dusty, gravel roads. Everything they did with her was a big adventure. I wish they could remember, but they were too young.

My daughter missed out on fun with her grandmother. I try to keep her alive as I tell the kids stories about my life with her. Not everything I have to share is positive, but who can say that about any relationship. I often wonder what life would be like if she was still around, but like those golden leaves in the meadow, she is gone.

My dad is still alive. I spend as much time with him as I possibly can. We are very close. Over the years we have had many happy memories. Every Saturday, my sisters, Glenda and Tracy and I spend the day with him. We have lunch and listen to old classic country music. Sometimes dad will get out his guitar and we will sing for him. We enjoy the time we get to spend with each other. My brother Jack comes when he can, but his job keeps him away a lot.

My dad has a wonderful sense of humor. He is always finding things to say to make us laugh. My children and grandchildren have had the honor of getting to know him. I love that! My youngest grandson will come in and go right up to him, insisting on dad picking him up and he will grab dad's ear and hang on for a minute, as if to say are you listening? It's so cute.

I know that these days will be gone way too fast so I savor every moment with my family. It is one thing that brings me joy more than anything else except of course the time I get to spend with the Lord.

My prayer is that everyone in my family will come to know the Lord in relationship with Him, so that we can continue to enjoy our time with each other in eternity, because, you can live forever, but not here!

Psalms 144:4 "Man is like a breath; His days are like a passing shadow."

I will take the day that I've been given and enjoy it as if it were the only one.

My Little Hero

I CAN REMEMBER IT LIKE it was yesterday. It was a very proud moment in my life. My youngest son Bryan should have gotten the Brave Medal of Honor. It was in the middle of the day and the kids were in school. My oldest son Jason came in the house telling me a story of an old man lying in the back alley. He thought the guy was playing a trick on him, so he ran around him, coming home to tell me as fast as he could.

I must confess that I didn't know my neighbor very well. We had just moved into our neighborhood and I really wasn't much for introducing myself and making myself friendly as I should.

Just as soon as my older son got finished telling me about his little incident with the stranger in the back alley, my younger son can running in to the house telling me quite a different story about the man lying in the alley.

He called 911because he thought there was something wrong with the man. Sure enough, the man was sick and had a stroke. The e-squad came and took the guy to the hospital. My son was so excited that he got the opportunity to help someone that he beamed with delight. It wasn't that he wanted there to be anything wrong with the guy, but he very possibly saved this guy's life.

I was so proud of my son that I was busting at the seams. In the meantime there stood my other son who had been quite paranoid. I was proud of him too. He had done what I had always told him to do and that is to not trust strangers. He was looking at it in a completely different perspective. What if the man would have been playing a trick on him and had been a pedophile. You can never be too careful. Yet sometimes we have to follow our gut feeling. My son's gut was telling him that this guy was legitimate and was in danger and needed some help. I was so proud of both of them and I wanted them to know it. My children were growing up to be mighty men of Valor. Both seeing different in their eyes, but both being right.

I often wonder what God thinks of us and our perspective. Does He get a big kick out of the way we sometimes solve our problems, when we go about it a different way than He does? Yet it is so important to have the ability to see things God's way.

Many times I have read the Bible and never really understood what the Father was saying. Years later I look at the same words that I have read year after year, and all of a sudden, I am getting a whole new perspective, as I look at what I'm reading through the eyes of the Father, it brings a whole new meaning. I just wonder why I didn't see it the same way before now. It actually was hidden from my eyes as though God had to wait to see if I would be longsuffering and responsible enough to do something with what I was seeing and hearing.

This week it happened that way. I have read Mark 4:24 I don't know how many times. For the first time I read it in a whole new light. I was so excited to see God's perspective that I'm still beside myself. It begins like this: "Then He said to them,(His disciples) Take heed what you hear. With the same measure you use, it will be measured to you; and to you who hear, more will be given". (Verse 25) "For whoever has, to him more will be given; but whoever does not have, even what he has will be taken from him."

This all of a sudden, at least for me, changes everything. I can't just read the Word of God and do nothing with it! I must do something or I will lose it and nothing more will be given to me. I can't begin to tell of the things that were going through my mind when I realized the times I've read the Word of God and didn't respond, or do something with what I read. Its ok, I'm only accountable for the things I know. So because He has showed me this I now am accountable. But how many people has He tried to show this to that hasn't gotten it? After all, we don't have the Bible for simply a reading enjoyment. It is a sword, a life manual. It's alive!

Now, I must spread this word to others and I have to wonder what kind of a response that I will get when I do. I must be careful to plant this seed in good ground that none of it falls into bad soil. For whoever hears it and does nothing with It, will now become accountable for what they know if they have a clear understanding.

My youngest son knew in his heart that there was a problem. If he would have just kept on walking, it could have been a catastrophe. He was led to doing something because I believe the Holy Spirit put the red flag inside him to know to do something right then and there. The man lived and rewarded my son with a complete set of encyclopedias. You would have thought my son had been given a million dollars.

On the other hand, my oldest son did not get that signal and was unaware of the true problem that man was having. He was not accountable for walking by. I feel this happened to teach us all a lesson on this very issue. If we pay attention God will speak to us daily in His word, the things He wants us to learn.

I wonder what will be done with the information we are given.

"But he who did not know, yet committed things deserving of stripes, shall be beaten with few. For everyone to whom much is given, from him much is required; and to whom much is committed, of him they will ask the more." Luke12:48.

Bon Appetite

LET'S TAKE A LOOK BACK in time for a moment. In a twinkling of an eye, Life turned on me and I had no idea how it all really came about. It's good to remember the bad once in a while, just to make sure you don't forget it. Things happen, it's not a pretty picture but it's my life all the same. It's like slipping on ice, one minute you are walking and the next thing you know, you are lying flat on your back thinking, what just happened?

Most addicts I know have an appetite for anything they are not allowed to have, and I am no exception. I love to put things into my system that causes me the greatest harm. Alcohol is a deadly choice for me. I love the way it burns my chest as it flows into my bloodstream. At first it makes me happy, then, it makes me sad. After about the fourth drink I want to fight and then I cry. Although I understand what the end result of my drinking will be, I still desire to do it.

When the effects of my addiction wreaked havoc on me, in a way that could have ended my life, I decided to change it. No longer was there a pay-off, because I continued my use for a different reason than when I first began. I was no longer using for the fun of it. I began depending on it to make it through rough times. I knew I had to do something different, or I would die young.

Sometime between the time I turned a teenager and the time I got married, I really screwed up my life. I went from having everything in control to being helpless. I don't think even my parents had a clue as to what was happening to me.

I began taking inventory of my life the night I overdosed on valium and drank a case of beer. The year was 1981. I ended up handcuffed to hospital bed, in Hearn, Texas. I was so humiliated when I realized that everything was now going to be out in the open. No longer would I be able to pretend that everything in my life was normal. Actually everyone but a few already knew, but I was in denial. Maybe it was time to take a good look at all the things I had wanted to hide. Things like a low self-esteem, lust, insecurity, my using, and the list went on and on. I also needed to take a moral inventory of myself. Where were all my morals? What were some of my character defects? How could I be so wretched? Was there anything more important to me than using? I was a liar, a cheat, I would steal when I needed to, I hated, I manipulated. I was a bad person. Did I do the things I did because I used, or did I use because I did the things that were bad? I couldn't be sure, but I knew neither was good.

All of these things I thought about had a common bond. They were the threads that made up my life. They were all part of my shortcomings. I hated having them, but couldn't see me getting rid of any of them any time soon. I did eventually change things, but it took a long time.

I revisit them once in a while. It's kind of like getting in your car and driving down the road, knowing you must look in your rear-view mirror once in a while just to keep things in check. If I look back constantly I will have an accident. It's the same way with my life, I don't dwell on the past, but I do remind myself that I have one, just to keep me humble. I tend to look back on those days when I feel sad or lonely, depressed or angry. If I'm not careful, those things will take me to places I don't need to go. If I regain my appetite for the lust of the flesh, I will reap a harvest of bad fruit.

I'm still capable of behaving badly. My old sin nature is still a part of my make-up. It is the good, bad and the ugly of my life. That doesn't change until I die. I manage that part rather well. Although occasionally it rears its ugly head then I have to starve it, so it will weaken. It reminds me of a poem a lady from Hot Springs Arkansas used to quote to me;

Two natures lie with-in my breast,
One is cursed, and one is blessed.
One I love, and one I hate.
The one I feed will dominate.

That's where my Higher Power comes in. He gives me the strength to say no. No to the lies, to the cheating, to the stealing, all the dirt that has caused scars to form on my heart. He forgives me for all I have done. I've been transformed. My goal is to live the next fifty years, bringing as much glory to His name, as I did shame in the first fifty.

I would like to say that I put all the right things into my body these days, but that would be a lie. But I have come a long way. I eat better, I'm not a liar anymore, I don't steal, I quit cheating, and I feed the nature that is blessed. I

12

guess that's called growing! Thirty years I've been in the making, and God's not done with me yet.

Psalms 34:8, "O taste and see that the Lord is good."

The Bean Whore

I'M NOT SURE WHEN THE place where I work opened, I'm thinking close to twenty-five years ago. The people who make up the staff, very quickly earned my respect. What I have discovered here, is a dedicated treatment team that goes beyond the call of duty to care for fragile, broken, lost souls, without hope.

I never see the doors close. We are open around the clock, all year long. There have been many times the count has been low, but rarely have I ever seen the place without a client. I can always depend on the sickness of drug abuse and alcoholism to keep us in business.

There has been a motley crew, grace our doors. Lawyers, doctors, prostitutes, house wives. Addiction is never a respecter of persons. I open my arms to "who so ever will." I would like to say I remember ever client that has walked through the doors but that's not true. There have been too many and that's sad, but true.

One that stands out to me more than the rest, is a client I call "the bean whore." I call her that not because I'm being disrespectful, but because that's a name we have reserved for each other as a result of an intimate moment we shared, changing the way we interacted with each other for the remaining time of her stay. She took root and bloomed.

She rolled on the floor laughing, until she couldn't catch her breath. It had been a long time since she was able to let go. There is nothing funny about addiction, but recovery should be gut-busting. We were watching a comedian on a video, brought in to the facility by another client. The comedian was a former addict and knew how to get the attention of an audience that was broken, bruised, used up, and too scared to show any emotion. This comedian was gifted. He was clean and sober and somehow his sense of humor was still intact.

I watched the client sit there, looking for a way to remove the guard she had placed upon her heart. We were chuckling at just about everything this comedian was saying. I could relate to his experiences in a way that a non-addict could not, and I knew she could too.

Then something magical happened. The dam broke, and when it let go, it didn't stop. She couldn't stop laughing. We were laughing at the fact that the only addiction this comedian had left was caffeine. For an addict, caffeine is not considered an addiction.

Like a nurse preparing to take blood, the comedian took the microphone cord and proceeded to wrap it around his arm, slapping his vein. He looked into the audience as if they were a counter clerk at a popular coffee house. He then proceeded to say the words that set this girl rolling on to the floor. "Give it to daddy bean whore!" The tears came, the laughter exploded, the moment was priceless. You would have had to been there.

Up until then, she had always put on a public smile, a manipulating voice and a pleasant demeanor, but those things did not inner-lock with her private self. In order to be emotionally and mentally healthy, the private self and public self at least have to touch. I'm not saying those didn't connect for her, but it was a far cry from being an eclipse. Laughter had been the medicine of the day. From then on, I saw her differently.

I would like to tell you that she was one of the one's that stayed clean but the "bean whore" has relapsed. My hope is that she will find her way back into treatment before it's too late. I bid her happiness and sobriety.

When I'm sitting in my office at the end of the day, and I hear in the living room a group of girls coming together and laughter is the common bond that they share, it makes me smile. They give off the sound of hope when that happens, knowing that just a short time before, they had no hope and absolutely nothing to laugh for. Thank God for places that will give people another chance.

Proverbs 15:13 "A merry heart makes a cheerful countenance, But by sorrow of the heart the spirit is broken."

Preparing for War

ADDICTION HAS THE POTENTIAL TO drag your soul off to hell. Many people give up without a fight and wonder why they are sucked into a vacuum of unending torment.

There is a weapon that can be used to battle this disease. In fact it has the power to bring addiction to its knees. The word "no" is the most powerful tool an addict can possess. Although it's rare when a person imprisoned by addiction wants to use it. The thought of never getting to experience the high you spend your whole life searching for, isn't exactly tempting. That's why addiction seems to be winning.

Like it or not, we all are part of this war on addiction. The question is, will we be participators or will we take the role of a spectator? Regardless of whether I'm in active addiction or not, my tax payers' dollars are still going to fight this disease. If I can get the client to intervene at the first thought of using, and use the tools provided them to exercise not picking up, I won't see the same clients returning year after year for another try at sobriety. What I will see is, healthy clients that have learned to manage their addiction, jumping on the band wagon to help others by paying it forward, sharing their experience in recovery, and as a result, maybe pay less out of my paycheck, because these ones have finally got it.

One thing that makes this disease bearable is the fact that we are not alone in the fight. A war is made up of many soldiers, each one with the armor and equipment to fight an enemy that will not fight fair. I have learned early on, that the key to my sobriety is to bring every thought I think, to the forefront for examination to see what the end result of that thought will bring. If it breeds life, it gets to go from a thought to an action, if it breeds death, it goes before a firing squad in my mind and I execute it before it brings harm to me or others. I must train my brain to execute every thought in my imagination. If a client of mine remembers nothing else, my hope is that they will remember to intervene.

In 1982 a woman by the name of Helen Hawthorne gave up the fight and went to her final resting place after losing her battle with addiction. I watched her year after year struggle to free herself from the clutches of her strong opponent. She was a beautiful wife, a loving mother, (my mother) a great gardener and a wonderful cook. I could fill the page with things she was good at. At one point I allowed my own addiction to blind me of the good things I wanted to remember her by. All I could think of was the times I saw her in her active addiction, not knowing or understanding until I became a drug and alcohol counselor, what it was that made her do the things she did.

One thing that I have learned in my profession is that alcohol and drugs mess up the part of the brain that is responsible for making good decisions. I couldn't realize until it was too late, that she was unable to make right decisions and as a result of that, I harbored great resentment toward her that kept me very sick for a long period of time. Had I not entered the field of addiction counseling I would have probably gone to my grave hating her, but God in His mercy, would not allow that to happen. Addiction took from me, the best part of my life with her. I feared her, I desired her love and affection, but that was something she wasn't capable of giving to me. What I now know is that she did love me and cared for me and was paralyzed from showing it. Preoccupied and blind-sided, she never knew that the love of her life (alcohol) was the very thing that would lure her to her death.

My God is the God of second chances, therefore I believe that when I knock at Heavens door my mother will be one in those great cloud of witnesses the Bible talks about that cheer us on. I believe that she will be there to welcome me home and we will have a chance to get to share the love that was taken from us at the hands of our addiction.

I made amends with my mother at her grave site years ago. I told her that I forgive her and know she was not at fault. I believe very strongly that, if she would have known what could have been done, she would have moved Heaven and Earth to do it.

I would be a fool to think that I have all the answers, if that were true, I would never see a client repeat a stay. One think is for certain, this disease is unpredictable. I do know that I'm on the front lines of battle and if I can't win this war on addiction, I can at least give it my best shot trying. Will I win? That remains to be seen. Will I gladly hand over the reins to the One who can? I already have.

2 Corinthians 10:5 "Casting down arguments and every high thing that exalts itself against the knowledge of God, bringing every thought captive

to the obedience of Christ, and being ready to punish all disobedience when your obedience is fulfilled."

I have learned to intervene and bring every thought safely to the cross.

Danger on the "High" Way

THE SOUTHBOUND LANES ON INTERSTATE 70 have two seasons, winter and construction. I have traveled that road for a period of years, transporting my children back and forth to their father. As often as I have driven it, I never once thought of all the other people who travel that road and how many are under the influence as they drive. When I think of all the deaths caused by drunk drivers, it petrifies me to think that my children and grandchildren travel those roads. What's even more frightening, I have two sons who are truck drivers and earn a living by being out on the road.

I could lay money on the fact that they too have been under the influence of some kind of substance as they try hard to meet the dead lines to get their freight delivered on time. I know this because they are my children and have the same DNA that runs through my veins. This makes them candidates for addiction. If I was to ask them how many times they drove under the influence, they would want to lie to me and protect me from knowing the truth. I do know the truth and it's not a pretty picture. I don't want to believe that my sons are plagued with this horrible sickness, but the odds are not in their favor.

I used to sit up at night when my children were still at home worrying myself sick, knowing if the phone rang it could be someone calling to tell me that one of my kids had been hit by a drunk driver or had hit someone while under the influence. I'm not sure what would hurt the most.

Sometimes I want to be in denial and choose to believe that my off spring is smart enough not to drink and drive .Until lately, I didn't understand that the brain continues to grow until the age of about 25. If you are drinking at an early age, the brain is affected in such a way that you don't think ahead of what the consequences can be as a result of using. When I was my children's age, I just wanted to have fun with my peers. I wasn't trying to get away with anything I just wanted to fit in.

I've stopped traveling Interstate 70, at least for the same reasons I used to. Now if I'm going somewhere I am always aware that there are untold users flooding the highways. I took a defensive driving class to help me know what to look for when I do travel. I think it has paid off. I don't want to be like an ostrich with my head in the sand any longer. I want to know what I'm up against. As for my boys, I'm choosing to believe that they are mighty men of valor. I know one day they will be working against those who choose to pick up a drink and drive.

Isaiah 5:11 "Woe to those who rise early in the morning, that they may follow intoxicating drink."

I have known that woe.

Unpredictable

Not even two weeks after I moved in with my sister, the biggest storm I've ever been in, moved through our neighborhood. I had just put my grandson in his car seat and before I had a chance to get out of the back seat into the front, I was dripping from my head to my toes. I sat there waiting for the rains to stop and as I waited, I realized that we were in the middle of what appeared to be a tornado.

My business partner told me that the radio towers by her parents' house that have been there since 1932 collapsed in this storm. I found out later that they were supposed to withstand winds up to 120 miles an hour. The towers came very close to falling on her parents' house.

The trees around my sisters' house, was uprooted and destroyed with-in seconds. The highway I took to get to work that evening had evidence of tornado activity that devastated several small areas in our neck of the woods. We were without power for several days.

This type of damage is very unusual for the place we live. I'm 50 and only once or twice since I was a child have I heard of anything like this happening.

Drinking is like that sometimes. You never expect it to do the damage it does. Back in the day, I never expected it to hit me so hard. I would be drinking one minute and the next thing I know I couldn't walk a straight line. My intentions were to quit before I was out of control but it didn't happen that way.

I've been clean thirty years, except for one night about ten years ago. I thought I could take a drink and stop. I thought I could drink sensibly and no-one would notice that I was having a drink. My son had not been old enough to remember my drinking days. He thought it was funny to see his mother with a drink in her hand and thought it kind of cool.

I took the first drink and nothing happened. I thought to myself, "I got this." I took my second drink and still nothing. By the time I drank half a bottle of homemade wine, I was plastered. It hit all at once. One minute I felt nothing (except for the burning in my chest as it went down) the next thing I knew my head was spinning and I could hardly walk. I decided we should finish the night up at the local bar just once for old time sake, but I never made it there. A friend of mine took me by my house to change cloths and I couldn't make it back out the door. She told me to lie down on my bed but keep one foot on the floor so I wouldn't spin. (Good advice) I woke up the next morning so sick I thought I was going to die. For the next three days I was so sick that I swore I would never drink again, and I haven't. I found out since then, that the reason I was so sick was that I had alcohol poisoning. The amount of alcohol that I had consumed in that short amount of time could have killed me.

Like the storm that came quickly, was my decision to pick back up and drink. I didn't see the end result coming. It just came out of nowhere kind of like that tornado. Alcoholism is at best unpredictable. When you decide to drink, you can jump back on the wagon, or you could find yourself drinking mouthwash and living out of your car. I was fortunate. I jumped right back on the wagon and have been riding smooth for the last ten years.

My sister is still cleaning up the mess from the storm, and I'm still cleaning up the mess left behind from my years of drinking. Her yard will one day be free of all the debris. The lives that I have affected will never be debris free.

Psalms 107:27-31 "They reel to and fro, and stagger like a drunken man, and are at their wits end. Then they cry out to the Lord in their trouble, and He brings them out of their distresses. He calms the storm, So that its waves are still. Then they are glad because they are quiet; So He guides them to their desired haven. Oh that men would give thanks to the Lord for His goodness, and for His wonderful works to the children of men! Let them exalt Him also in the assembly of the people, and praise Him in the company of the elders."

Thank you Lord that I am sober today, enjoying every benefit that You have given me.

The Extraordinary

GOD HAS BEEN SPEAKING TO me in words. I wake up in the morning and I hear a word spoken to me and it will be highlighted in my mind. Most of the time the highlighted word isn't a group of words spoken, it is one word that leads to a treasure of events that I get to explore throughout the day. By the end of the day I am able to put everything together like a beautiful 3-D puzzle.

As I do word studies, I realize that the word is a direction that I am supposed to go in. I get excited when I am summoned to search these words out to see what is being spoken to me. Most of the time, I can look back and see where God chose to push me in a direction I would not have normally traveled.

Just recently, the word, "extraordinary" was spoken by a pastor who I love to listen to. This pastor is a man who gets excited about life and all that God has for him and his family. His passion is contagious. When I listen to him, he encourages me to step out of my comfort zone, into the unexpected and enjoy encounters that I would, no doubt miss, if left to myself.

For instance, when I picked up the Webster's dictionary to hunt up the word extraordinary, I opened the dictionary to the very page that held that word. Now, that to me is extraordinary. Normally I wouldn't have picked up that book because I have a dictionary on my laptop that I use when I am writing. I don't have a Webster's dictionary, so it would have been impossible for me to pick it up and use it if I was home. It just happens that right now, I don't have a home. I had to move out of my apartment because of mold issues that the company I rent from refuses to deal with. My apartment was flooded about a month ago, (twice in one week) and I began experiencing problems because of the mold, so I moved out. Now you may ask, "What's that have to do with anything." Well, I have been staying with my sister who has been a blessing to me. I'm not sure if she has a Webster's dictionary or not. She probably does, but that's not the one that I picked up to do the word study with.

I have another sister who has ask me to house sit for her while her and her husband vacations in Canada. She has her dictionary sitting out on her coffee table where her bible usually sits, probably because she has taken her bible with her on her trip, and she wanted her coffee table to looked like it usually does, (occupied by books.) In this series of events that I want to share with you, you will be able to see an extraordinary group of happenings that took place in order to actually pick up that dictionary to the exact word I was looking up.

If the dictionary was not on her table this morning, and had the Lord not given me that exact word… and had I missed the word…or if it had not been highlighted in my mind this morning…. and if I would have gotten through to a friend I had tried to contact all morning long… and if I hadn't sat down to write, trying to meet a dead line I have put on myself… I would not have picked up the Webster's dictionary and opened it up to the word I was searching for. To me that's extraordinary.

I feel like I was pushed through to that series of events to show me that God officiates over the everyday affairs of His people. Now, I believe that He could let me go through my life, in the boring everyday ordinary, but He is so much more fun than that. Now, if I want, He would probably leave me to my wretched self, though He knows me better than I know myself and it brings me great pleasure for Him to rule over my affairs and I give Him permission every day to do just that. I think He wants me to experience extraordinary things in my life.

When I finally read what extraordinary means, I had to laugh. The first thing I read was, "out of course." That to me was breath taking. Then it said, "Going beyond what is usual, regular or customary, exceptional to a very marked extent, remarkable, beauty, employed for, or sent on a special function, or service." The last thing it said was, "an ambassador!" I was blown away. I knew the day was going to be fun. I was anticipating the most unusual day. It had already started and if it doesn't get any better than this, the day is already extraordinary. I know that this is a minute subject to get so excited about, but the point is that no matter how small or big things happen in your life, we must know that God thinks they are important.

Proverbs 3:6 "In all your ways acknowledge Him, and He will direct your paths."

I know the Lord wants me to know extraordinary.

Fault Lines

THE CHURCH HAD BARELY ENOUGH people to keep it open. Although it had 6 times more than what it had when the pastor took it over. A special speaker was giving the message, because our pastor had to be out of town to serve communion at a church that has recently lost its pastor.

It was a beautiful day, the sun was shining, and the temperature had not risen to the height that made our un-air-conditioned tiny country church unbearable to sit in. I sat there hoping the God of the whole universe would have a place of honor, having the glory due His name, in-spite of the lack of congregational members that were missing. Our little piece of heaven, in the middle of no- where use to be a booming place to be, on Sunday mornings.

At times you can count the people that show up on one hand. There are not enough children to have Sunday school or children's church and it's almost a waste of time to have Sunday school for the adults, but we do.

Something has happened. I don't pretend to know what it is because I'm not from this area. This particular morning as I listened to the message, I thought I might have had a teeny peak at what could have been going on. The sweetest lay-speaker in the world as far as I'm concerned proceeded to give a message that knocked me right off my seat, and she didn't even know anything was happening. She related to her congregation about the end times that the bible speaks about in Matthew and 2nd Peter. It was a reminder of the things to look for as our world uncontrollably spirals out of control. In the midst of the conversation, she happened to mention a movie, her and her husband had watched on the end of the world. The topic of earthquakes came up because it's one of the signs of the times. She spoke specifically about the fault lines that run through the United States and where they run. It was a warning, that one day we could experience devastation and would we be ready if that occurred.

Having a runaway brain as I do, I immediately began to think about those fault lines. I believe at some time in the past I might have even heard someone else preaching about it. I thought about how our very beings were made up of the earth, and we too are not perfect and can have fault lines inside us, much like the earth. Secret places that are forming, psychotic breaks and matters of the heart that keep us from living as we should.

I've experienced fault lines. For many years I dealt with the sin of lust. I would flirt with it and do things that no one was aware that I was doing, except for the people I was flirting with. I didn't cross over the lines, but the lines seemed to be growing bigger and bigger as the days went by, just like the fault lines we have in the earth here in the U.S.

It wasn't until my world came crashing down around me and my family lay in ruins, that I was able to admit that I had a problem. By then, it was too late to do anything about it. Had I done the right thing in the beginning, and allowed someone to know and help me with the problems I was having I might not have had to lose my family as a result. I could have moved away from the sin and gave it over to the one who could do something about it. I chose to handle it myself because I didn't want anyone to know I had that problem. I was embarrassed and ashamed, and it cost me dearly.

I wish I could say that lust was the only thing I had ever had to deal with. My drug habit was the same way. For years no one knew I had a problem. Inside of me, the fault line was getting bigger and bigger and no one knew it. Eventually my world was in small pieces all around me and others were expected to pick up the pieces and go on.

I believe all addicts have those same fault lines. Until we get help and start managing our addiction, we are at risk for our world to come to destruction. Much like the people who monitor the fault lines under the United States, we too can watch and manage the fault lines underlying with-in us. Even though there is nothing that can be done to prevent them from being there, we might want to explore options, that will reduce the probability of the number of people that will get hurt as a result of any personal earthquake that might take place because of them.

I want, and do monitor my life on a daily basis, trying to do the "next right thing" so that my world and those who live in it will no longer be hurt because I refused to take responsibility for my actions.

I want to thank the ones who are bold enough to remind me that it is necessary for me to do that often, even when they don't know they are doing it.

Psalms 66:18 "If I regard iniquity in my heart, the Lord will not hear."

Psalms 32:5 "I acknowledged my sin to you, and my iniquity I have not hidden. I said, "I will confess my transgressions to the Lord," and you forgave the iniquity of my sin."

The earthquake is over, the tremors have ended and He has rebuilt the ruins of my life!

Angel's Trumpets

ON THE SIDEWALK CLOSE TO my dad's apartment, stands a flower known as Angel's trumpet. I'm not sure how it came about to be called that, possibly because the flowers are the shape of trumpets or because they are deadly. If it is because they are deadly, then they are probably called that, because in the bible, it talks about when the angel's blow their trumpets, the dead in Christ will rise and those who remain will be caught up together in the air to meet the Lord and we will forever be with Him. In order for that to happen, I think we have to die, either to our flesh or literally. Probably both but regardless, death is involved either way.

This plant, whose scientific name is called Datura, is a plant belonging to the Solanaceae family. According to Wikipedia encyclopedia, "Most parts of the plant contain toxic hallucinogens having a long history of use, for causing delirious states and death. It was well known as an essential ingredient of love potions and witches' brews."

"Children are especially vulnerable to atropine poisoning and their prognosis is likely to be fatal. In some parts of Europe and India, Datura has been a popular poison for suicide and murder." People have actually tried to put this in stews and ended up in the hospital because of it. (I read this in article on Datura from the internet. The article goes on to say, "No other substance has received as many train wreck reports as Datura. The overwhelming majority of those who describe their use of Datura find their experiences extremely mentally and physically unpleasant and often physically dangerous."

One thing I'm surprised about is that I haven't heard any of my clients talk about this drug. Either they don't know it's out there, or they call it by another name. Drug addicts are always looking for something new to take. It doesn't matter if the plant kills you or not, some addicts I know would just have to stand up to the challenge to see if they could take it without dying. Some would take it hoping that they would die, so they would be put out of their misery. Others would sell it on the streets, not caring if it took someone else's life.

I'm thankful that even though there are deadly substances out there that can take my life, I have protection, when I'm in God's care that keeps me from danger.

Mark 16:18 "They will take up serpents; and if they drink anything deadly, it will by no means hurt them; they will lay hands on the sick and they will recover."

Caterpillars and Butterflies

LATELY I'VE BEEN NOTICING BEAUTIFUL butterflies. I see them everywhere. I see them flying above the fields out over the beautiful country side. I see them in our back yard. I've noticed them around the garden and on pretty flowers, but seeing them on the road when I'm driving to my dad's house has been unexpected. The road is a state route and it's quite busy, so to actually see these fluttering little creatures flittering around and sometimes flying into the cars that are rushing by, really makes me wonder why they are there.

It's not a combination of different species I see. These butterflies are small, black, and there are a lot of them. Some of them have been run over. For years it seemed rare to me to see just a couple of them in and around the same place, so for me to be seeing so many, and to the point that they are getting run over, really has gotten my attention.

When I think of butterflies, it makes me also think of caterpillars. Then when I think of caterpillars, I think of the terrible fear my oldest son had of them when he was four. One day I tried to get him to go outside and play. When he opened the front door, there were several of these creepy crawlers exploring our entry way. Jason simply came back inside and shut the door. I insisted that he go out- side and play with the other kids. He informed me that he was not going to go out because of the aterpillars. (He couldn't pronounce the word properly.)

I look back on that day with much regret. Instead of having an understanding heart, I yelled at him because he was afraid. I wasn't the kindest parent and I was so self-absorbed because of my addicted life, that I felt no empathy or concern for anything or anyone except me. I thought it was ridiculous that he was a boy and was scared of a little caterpillar. If I could go back to that day, I would have scooped him up in my arms and reassured him that I would never allow him to be in harm's way. I would have taken the creepy crawlers and relocated them somewhere else in the yard. It could have been a bonding moment for me and my son, but I ruined the opportunity, and know that I will never get another chance, at least not with that situation, to make it right. I have thought about that moment many times since, and each time it makes me sad that I missed a chance to save the day.

I'm not now, who I was back then. I'm thankful to say that today I have become less self- absorbed and am a very caring person. My children look at me in amazement with the way I treat my grandchildren and they wonder what happened to the woman I once was. I may not be able to turn back time and relive that day, but I can let my children and grandchildren know that I would die for them if need be now, and I don't say that lightly.

I see women in early recovery react the same way I used to. It's easy to be focused on self when you are just coming out of active addiction. I tell them they remind me of caterpillars. Once they begin their journey to recovery it will be like coming out of a self- spun cocoon. There is a big unexplored world out there. If given the opportunity, they can fly around like the tiny black butterflies I've been seeing all over the place. Once the cocoon is broken, and freedom from addiction is reached, the sky is the limit, I know, I've been there.

My son is all grown up now. He's no longer afraid of caterpillars. I still want to scoop him up and tell him everything is going to be alright, because there are still a lot of scary things outside his door.

Romans 12:2 "do not be conformed to this world, but be ye transformed by the renewing of your mind."

The Dance of the Leaves

My favorite time of year is autumn. I love to get into my car and drive to my favorite back roads where I can find the ones that have the most fallen leaves. It takes my breath to watch in the rear-view mirror as I observe the brilliant colored leaves get tossed into the air and then float gently back down onto the ground.

I have mixed emotions as I participate in this yearly event. I can't wait for fall to begin, and yet there is a lingering sadness all around me as I think about how short lived this brief interlude is. If it wasn't for the fact that I know it's special because of its fleeting moment, I would ask God to let autumn last all year long.

I can't prove it, but I think that Jesus was born in the fall. Every year at this time I get the Christmas Spirit. I thought at first it was because the Lord wanted to give me a gift, or that something special was going to happen closer to Christmas and I would need to know about it before it happened. Now, I think it is because it is the true time the Lord was born.

I live close to a lake and often go there to sit and stare at the beautiful trees that slowly turn into a kaleidoscope of fall colors from the end of September through the end of October and if I'm lucky half way through the month of November.

I also love the sun when it dances off the lovely blue water. Watching the two together is a special treat. I wonder at times how people can see things like this every day of their lives and not know that there is a God in the heavens that created everything that has been created.

I talk to people every day that are unaware, until they get sober, that there is such beauty. They tell me they are seeing things for the first time. It's sad that they have spent so much of their life missing out on simple little things like, a yellow bird or a blooming flower.(I know that I haven't always appreciated those dancing leaves). Life for them is truly just beginning.

Ecclesiastes 3:1 "To everything there is a season, a time for every purpose under the heavens."

"If retribution fails as a value, perhaps there exists some mystical cosmic order that grants meaning to life, for each thing has its proper time or cycle." (Unknown).

Intervene at the First Thought

THE TATTOO WAS SMALL. You could hardly read it. It may be the only one like it. It sat at the bend of her arm. It was put there to constantly remind her not to use. It read, "Intervene at the first thought." "You must bring every thought captive." I probably said those words to her a hundred times. I would say to her, "If you never remember anything else that I say to you, don't forget to intervene at the first thought." It's not an easy thing to do. In fact, it's probably the hardest thing any addict will have to do. To say to an addict, "Don't pick up" is like saying to a fish, "don't go into the water". It's not easy but it is vital. I never thought she would tattoo those words to her arm. I also never thought she would pick-up again, but she did. Although she heard the word intervene, she somehow forgot the part where I told her that unless she wanted to stay clean, those words won't help. The sad truth is, relapse is more the norm then the exception.

If I would have waited until the temptation of using was there and then the obsession, it would have been too late to manage this monster. If I would not have managed it, it would have swallowed me up and I would have died. So, the question is, how did I manage the addiction? For me, that didn't mean I had to go to a meeting every day, or surround myself with positive people that encouraged me and told me that I could do it. It didn't mean I had to read the "Big Book" (put out by the founders of AA) It didn't mean I had to work the 12 steps. It didn't mean I had to find a sponsor or someone that would take the time to work the steps with me. It didn't mean I had to gather phone numbers of women who also fight the battle of addiction. It didn't mean I had to pick up the phone every day and talk to whoever would listen and care enough to cry with me when I cried and laugh with me when I laughed. Although, that's exactly what I tell my client's to do every day.

For me that's not what I did. Not because it doesn't work, but because

I wanted to focus completely on my Jesus. When I first got clean, I didn't know about all those things, and if it was those things that I would have had to know in order to stay clean I would have been in big trouble.

There were those like me, who didn't know about AA. For us it was our church that supplied the sponsor. (I've had mine for 30 years. She's the best). The Big Book I used wasn't the blue book used in AA. It is the book with all the answers. It's my instruction manual. The Bible. Our Higher Power wasn't a higher power, it was THE Higher Power!

The day I turned my will and life over to Jesus Christ, was the day that I was set free from the chains of addiction. I have never looked back or spent one day regretting my decision to let Him control my destiny. It sure worked for me. I didn't have to tattoo my arm to remind me to stay clean; I just needed to tuck the, "want to" into my heart.

2 Cor. 10:5 "Casting down arguments and every high thing that exalts itself against the knowledge of God, bringing every thought into captivity to the obedience of Christ and being ready to punish all disobedience when your obedience is fulfilled."

Where's the Chocolate?

I LOVE CHOCOLATE! IT MAKES me happy. I eat a lot of it when I get stressed. I would be lying if I told you there weren't days when I needed a truck load.

Anything that can happen here usually does. One of the most interesting things that I can think of is a spirit here at our facility or so some think by the name of Fred. I hear clients talk of him often. When their children come, they all say the same thing. The spirit is a black man. Some think it is a slave from the civil war days. One child said, "He don't scare me, he is nice". This kid saw the spirit from the yard. He grabbed his mother's head and spun it around so she could see what he was seeing. He said, "Look at the black man in the window." The child wasn't afraid but the mother was a little freaked out.

For some reason all the kids see him. There have been clients who say that they wake up in the middle of the night and their bed is shaking and it scares the crap out of them. I've worked here quite a while and I have yet to see him. If I ever do get to see him, I will really need the chocolate.

One little girl saw him and screamed a blood curdling scream, started running for her mother missing, the two large steps she cleared, as she jumped into her mother's arms. She called him a monster. She needed some chocolate too. Another child walked into the living room one day and asks me, "Why is that ghost here? Then walked over to the steps and ask, "why is that ghost going upstairs?" I really didn't know what to say.

Other things happen here, I work midnights once in a while and I have to take crisis calls. When I first started working as a counselor, it was intimidating. I was so afraid that I would say something to the person on the other end of the line that would throw them right over the edge. Those nights I ate lots of chocolate.

I kept getting calls from a client that was bent on tormenting me. She really needed community mental health; instead, she called me every single night I was on midnight shift. It was as if she knew my schedule. Come to find out, she called every night. I know this was a crisis hot line but she made me want to kill myself. I finally sent a fax to the big boss, telling him that something had to be done with her. I referred her to the mental health clinic in our area and she quit calling.

I expect something different every day when I show up for work. Every walk of life has passed through our doors. This includes some of the nicest people and some of the nastiest. Things that shocked me in the beginning now bore me to tears. For instance, the language is appalling. It really blows your mind when you hear a four year old drop the f-bomb. The look on my face must have been priceless the first time I heard it. It doesn't get better just because it comes out of the mouth of the adults. The most shocking of all is when you get so frustrated with the clients that you hear it come out of your own mouth. That's when you know it's time to look for big bags of chocolate. (or find another line of work).

I remember the last program director who was an ex minister. After working here awhile, she cussed like an old soldier. I never knew what was going to come out of her mouth after spending some time at our facility. I think about her a lot and wonder if she has the same problems at her new place of employment. I wonder if I need to send her a box of chocolate.

I have a relapse prevention group that I teach on Thursdays. I have an activity I do with candy where I have the client's build a house from the foundation up, I'm thinking about having the client's build one with chocolate.

Chocolate can't help our situations, but it makes the day a little sweeter.

Wesselle De La Pack

Sac a lac a dac a frack. Quack a mac a ttack a shack. Wack a hack a pack a cack. Rick a schick a frick a mick. Tick a wicka sick a pick. Sip a tip a crip a mick. Saw a mall afral ra shal. Sing a ring a ding a ling. Ping a thing a ding a ling. Walk a schock a frock a dock. Sap a pap a crap a hack. Gib a crib a tib a fib.

The words are not supposed to make sense. Not everything in life does, especially addiction.

The end

Even as We Speak

I'M HEARING THUNDER. I WATCH out the window and I know there is a terrible storm brewing. I see the warning signs and I wonder how long it will take to reach us. Sometimes the storms that seem the most threatening are the ones that blow over, and the ones you think are nothing, fool you.

It is the same way with the clients. Today I learned that a client died of an overdose three days ago. The last group I taught her was about realizing that you can die if you go back out and think you can pick up where you left off.

Her coining ceremony was just days away, and I wanted her to know the danger she was in. Everyone laughed, including her, as she put her hand in a box filled with uncooked chocolate cake mix. I was teaching a relapse prevention group. She unexpectedly stuck her hand in something she was blindsided by.

I will never forget the look on her face. It was as if she knew it was just a matter of time before this disease of addiction would catch up with her. It was one of those signs. She had the most sober look on her face. Here it is two and a half weeks later and she's dead! I'm shocked. I didn't see her as one that wouldn't make it.

A fellow employee reminded me of a saying, a program director here always said, "Some have to die so others can live." There are clients here that went through the program with this girl. They can't believe she is dead. Even as I write this information to you, I have to stop and give someone directions. They are coming to share about the night before she died. They were with her.

I would like to tell you this is an isolated case. It's not. Death comes too quickly to those who challenge their knowledge of this disease. Other clients speculate about how it happens, asking me if it's possible that because she had just been in rehab, that she might have felt so bad about knowing what not to do, that she felt it was hopeless to quit. Maybe that's why she just kept right on using until she went beyond what her body could take. She alone knows. The ones who ask, have a familiar look, knowing that they too, have felt and thought the same thing after relapsing. A light bulb moment has happened. Will it stop these clients from ever using again? God only knows.

I feel sadness. I keep thinking that I will get used to the shocking news of a client when they die, but I don't. I am asked not to get attached to clients for this very reason. I see them five days a week for eight hours a day. The time frame is anywhere from 90 days up to a year. Many remind me of someone I know. How do I separate myself from them? I wish I could but then I feel like that would be so cold.

The storm has ended. My sadness has not. I see her face in my mind's eye, even as we speak.

Romans 6:23 "For the wages of sin is death, but the gift of God is eternal life in Christ Jesus our Lord."

Erosions from Emotions

JUST LIKE ACID REFLUX THAT can burn holes into your esophagus, anger has burnt paths through the client's emotions. Anger is a legitimate and deadly emotion. Anger will eat you up if it's not focused into a positive direction. The motivation behind anger is usually understandable. Horror stories are told to me often of client's children being mistreated and often sexually abused.

Little children get things put where they should never be, by people who should never be allowed around them. Clients tell me that it steals from them. It keeps them prisoner to anger. Some never break free. Clients have to go before judges, trying to explain where they were, when their children were being molested. The fear grips them as the children are ripped from their arms, sent to places you expect are safe but are often not. I've seen the faces of mothers who get a call that the foster homes their children are in, are under investigation. Their children have been sexually molested and they are looking for another foster home to place them in.

Try to explain to a mother how her child, who has never been hurt while in her care, is now having to see a therapist because their foster sibling has molested her child. Or worse, try to explain to a mother that her 18 month old daughter has been accidently killed while in foster care. I can't seem to find a place to direct that anger!

Anger turned inward is depression. Many women who enter our facility don't have the energy to be angry. They turn the anger inward because they don't know what else to do with it. They are often medicated to get to other issues, but I'm not so sure that's the answer.

I'm not sure which I would rather see, someone angry or someone that hates. One woman had a plan that she was going to cut her abuser up into tiny little pieces. She showed no emotion when she talked about it. He tried to kill her. She was very serious about what she was going to do. One of the staff tried to talk her out of it. She had no intention of changing her mind. She was discharged soon after she made the statement.

One client was very vicious. She would tell stories of what she did to people she didn't like. She would urinate into shampoo bottles or urinate on people's toothbrushes. This girl had some serious issues. She was eroding.

Sometimes I think the devil himself walks through these doors. There are those who have issues with emotions and there are those who are just evil. I am happy to say that those are a small percentage. Those kinds of clients don't stay very long. They are usually weeded out before they get to the house. Occasionally, one will slip through the cracks. The girl obsessed with urine was one of those people. She was a very angry young lady.

Just recently, I worked with a girl who told me she was in the service. She said she served in Germany. One day she told me she had to deal with children who came running up to her unit with grenades strapped to them. She told me that she had to decide whether to protect the children or to protect her unit. She said she made the decision to shoot the children. Every year at the same time she deals with this issue, to the point that she can't sleep for days. She also shared with me that she had stabbed her step-father because he had sexually abused her for years. She had been sent to prison for it. She did her time but the memory will be with her forever. Many more painful memories haunt her in the night hours. I see the pain eating away at her and I don't know how to help her. We offer to refer her out and hope she would take the life line but she knows that in order to heal, she will have to feel the scars of the past. I don't know how to ask her to not be angry.

Later I found out that she may have been making some of this stuff up. She could have been having a psychotic break from reality. It's bad when our clients can't tell reality for fiction. We can only try to help and let them know that we are there to help.

Proverbs 15:1 "A soft answer turns away wrath, But a harsh word stirs up anger."

Trash In, Trash Out

I WANTED HER TO LOOK me in the eye, but she covered her face with her coat. It was pretty clear that she would rather be any place but where she was. The scar on her face was worn like a badge. My heart still sinks when I think of the stories she told me of how her dad would kick her in the face with his steel toe boots.

I wish I could say this was the only story I've heard like this, but it's not. I'm not sure which bothered me most; the story of him kicking her in the face, or her constant need of his approval. She loved him. She wanted so badly for him to love her.

I remember the night I brought in a bag of trash from the kitchen. It was filled with rotten fruit, eggs, onions and anything else I could find in the refrigerator that was past its expiration date. I had my group sit in a circle and I handed the bag to the girl on my left.

I asked her if she wanted to take a bite, and she squealed out a big "no way". She then handed it to the girl on her left and that girl handed it to the girl on hers. The bag finally found its way back around to my seat. No one wanted to partake. I ask why I had no takers. Everyone replied something different.

I then discarded the bag into the trash, and began talking to the girls about the way people treat them. I told them I was sorry for the way life had been for them. I explained that, they had the right not to except all the negative words spoken over them. It was time for the girls to begin believing something positive. This was a harder task then I thought it would be.

When you have been physically and emotionally beat up, it's easy to buy into what everyone says about you. When you hear something long enough, you begin to believe it. The girls were not use to hearing pleasant things about themselves. I asked each girl to say something nice about the girl on their right. As each one began to speak, I could see the uneasiness in their eyes. I knew they weren't buying what was being said. It was easy for the girls to accept the negative, but they truly couldn't respond to the positive things said about them.

Many clients come to our place without teeth and their hair is a mess from years of using. They don't care if they bathe or not. They have medical problems because they haven't taken care of themselves. Their self-esteem has been completely destroyed. They have no hope.

A good thing happens because of treatment, many leave with teeth, their medical problems have been addressed and self- esteem has been restored. I care about them and they know it. Some come back wide eyed and bushy-tailed. They have a smile on their face, often with a job and a new lease on life. I wish I could say that for all the clients, but that's just not the case.

I haven't heard from my client since she left the program. I hope she is able to restore her relationship with her dad and find the love she has wanted so badly. The scars will never go away but maybe the pain of the past will fade into the background enough for her to enjoy the life she has left.

Proverbs 23:7 "For as he thinks in his heart, so is he."

Dealing with Difficult People

I GO TO WORKSHOPS THAT are drug and alcohol related. When I first started going, I never knew what I was going to get myself into. I thought that all workshops were professional and no matter which one I attended, I would receive my money's worth and get educated on the subject at hand, not true.

I was very upset to find out that some of the training sessions out there are scams to get people to buy their product. I only get to attend places that give continuing education hours once a year and it's important to me to be able to pack as much into that time as I can. I don't want to waste my companies' money or my time, going places that are useless.

A co-worker and my-self decided to go to a workshop called "Dealing with Difficult people." Since I work with drug addicts and Alcoholics I figured it would be interesting get information that would be helpful in case I was ever to be confronted by a difficult client.(Ha Ha.) I actually deal with those people on a daily basis and I'm at times desperate for advice.

As we entered the room, we saw a table full of books and material but didn't really pay any attention to it. The people presenting were exceptionally sweet and very accommodating. There were pitchers of water and coffee for us to drink, mints for us to snack on and a folder with information about what qualifies as a difficult person.

Once we were there for a while, it didn't take long to figure out that the people that didn't want to buy the product they had for sell, were the "difficult people." They had set the workshop up in such a way that it was almost impossible to leave without being bullied into buying expensive material that we couldn't afford.

I could see the light bulb moment's people throughout the room were having as they realized what was going on. I was able to talk to some of them during break, and I'm happy to say that most of them left and wasn't intimidated by their scheme.

Addiction is a lot like this. When I first started using, I thought I was going to benefit from the drugs I was using. People were very generous about sharing their drugs. They knew it was just a matter of time before they could intimidate me into buying something I couldn't afford.

Drug dealers have a way of dealing with the people they sell to. If a front is made and you can't come up with the money to pay for the drugs you have been given. It's not uncommon to find someone at the bottom of a dumpster.

That actually happened to one of my client's sister. She was a twin. My client got the news while she was in treatment, that her sister had come up missing and no one had heard from her in a days. It wasn't long before they identified her body in a dumpster. Had this girl not been in treatment, she probably would have been found with her sister. It was bazaar to go to her funeral and see this clients sister laying there looking exactly like my client. For the client, it was like seeing herself laying there dead. It was almost more than she could stand.

I'm not sure what went wrong. Maybe she didn't pay for the drugs she got. Maybe she tried to pull one over on the drug dealer, who, by the way was arrested not long after they found her. I may never know why he killed her or what she did to make him want to deal with her this way. It's incomprehensible! They don't come more difficult than that.

What If?

I MUST HAVE ASKED THAT question to myself a hundred times. What if I had not chosen to do the things I've done? That question causes me to go back a long way. Let's see, where would I start? What if I had not remembered that at four years of age I bent down behind an overstuffed chair in my mother's living room and prayed for my grandparents who were just in an automobile accident that claimed their lives?

I've been told that the first memory you have, sets the stage for who you become. Since that was my first memory, it makes sense to me that I have a strong relationship with Jesus Christ. I can't remember anyone ever telling me about Him, and yet I've always known Him. Not that it's been easy for me to do all the things that should have been done, I haven't. What if I would have? Who would I have become? I look back and think it would have been impossible for me to do all the things that might have been required of me. I lived with family who didn't live a Christian life. Jesus Christ was a word, not a person to them. I heard His name on a regular basis but not the way it should have been taught to me.

What would my life have looked like if my parents would have been Christians? I probably wouldn't have gotten married and divorced 3 times. I probably wouldn't have the 3 beautiful children that I have or the 7 loving, awesome, grandchildren that I love ridiculously, in spite of the fact that I don't get to be with all of them. I probably wouldn't be living with my sister who I also adore, as I do the rest of my family. I tell people when it comes to my family we're like the mafia. We are very close.

What if I would have said no to Jesus? That's one thought that makes me cringe. I remember thinking what if He doesn't want me? That scared me more than me not accepting Him. Well it turned out just fine, He wanted me and I was glad of it. I think He got the short end of the stick but He doesn't seem to mind.

There are so many things that I could question in my life. The truth is; if I had to do it all again I wouldn't trade my life for anyone else's. I have been truly blessed and my journey with the Lord hasn't been perfect because of my bad decisions but still, it is mine. I've learned from my walk and have grown to be more careful in the decisions I make. I see myself as a beautiful gem of His, dug up out of the dark rich dirt of life. He has taken and put me under the knife for He is the lapidary. He is polishing me and preparing me for His kingdom. When He is finished with me, I will be exactly what He wants and All the "what if's" in the world, won't change that.

Malachi chapter 3 say's, "They shall be mine," "Says the Lord of hosts, on the day that I make them my Jewels."

His love is never ending.

The Rest Between the Notes

I DON'T KNOW MUCH ABOUT music, but I do know that it is the rest, that gives music its beauty. I think about the rest in my life and an amazing thing happens, it makes me glad for all the things that I have done without. Money comes to mind first. I don't think there's anyone out there who thinks that they ever have enough money. How much is enough? I have had very interesting things happen when I didn't have enough money.

I had just gotten saved and was struggling with the faith thing. Everyone around me was sharing with me about believing for things before I saw them come about. There was one time in particular I remember not having enough money to make my car payment. I had bought a car from one of those places where you make payments on a weekly schedule. If for some reason, I missed a payment, I knew they would come and repossess my car. I lived in the country, I had 3 young children and my husband was gone all week and I needed that car. It was Sunday and the car payment was due on Monday.

I had found a church about 10 miles from where I lived. I had been going there only a short time so I didn't know hardly anyone. I got up on that Sunday morning, got the kids dressed, and off to church we went. I was very happy to be there and I can't remember for sure, but I think I must have said to God under my breath, something like, "God I need your help. My car payment is due tomorrow and I don't know what to do." I hadn't been taught about paying my tithes and giving offerings, but I was doing just what I knew to do. Just about that time, a lady who was sitting in front of me turned around in the pew and said, "I'm not sure why you need this but, I know the Lord wants me to give this to you." She smiled as she handed me fifty dollars.

I was so excited I almost became a pew jumper that day. Fifty dollars don't seem like much today but back then, it was like a million dollars to me.

Ok maybe I'm exaggerating but it was the exact amount I needed for my car payment. I didn't know whether to shout for joy or sit there and cry because of the relief I felt. Had I not needed the money, it would have been a missed opportunity for God to show Himself mighty in my life. What a lesson in faith that was for me.

Since that day, I can tell you of many instances that God has taken my needs and turned them into lessons in faith. He has met every need in my life. Not always in the way I thought He would. He has gone beyond what I would have settled for. I've had groceries given to me when we needed food, He has caused people to fix my car when it was broken down. He has supernaturally kept me alive in accidents that should have killed me.

I know that going without is something that I don't like to do, but I would not give for the experiences that I got to be a part of, since I got saved. Has it kept me from always living the way I should? No. I really feel bad that I've made big mistakes. He has not let that stand in the way of His love for me. I know He on the just and the unjust. What I have learned is; when you line yourself up with His word and try to do right, He will move Heaven and Earth for you. That's a great lesson to learn.

I don't usually think of doing without when I think of the musical rest. It all blends together so that I didn't realize that it's the part that is not, that makes what is, so beautiful. That stands true in my life as well. It's the rest, the things that are not, that give God the chance to make my life so lovely.

Thank you Lord!

The Gladiator

I have watched the "Gladiator" over and over again and every time I watch It, I see things in it, that I don't remember seeing before. I'm not one to watch war movies, so I never thought that I would be so consumed by watching this movie over and over.

The star of the show seems to have a determination that I want. He doesn't die easily, and when he does finally die, he has something to look forward to. He has given all he has, and has accomplished what he set out to do. He possesses a passion for the ones he loves, and fights to the end for them.

I had a vision one night. I was crawling on the ground in full combat gear with others to the right of me. I was very aware that I was on a mine field and my job was to disarm the mine's, that were hidden in that field. It was almost dark and it was hard to see what I was doing. I had no way of knowing were the live mines where, but I was sure that if we didn't disarm them, the ones who were coming behind us, would never make it.

I was moving very slow. Although it wasn't because I was fearful, for I somehow knew we were going to be ok. All of a sudden, a great wind began to blow and the sand that was covering the mine's, were all uncovered. I was able to deactivate the weapons that were meant for our destruction. It mattered to me that those that I loved were no longer going to be in harm's way.

I knew this vision was significant. I was being called to battle. Not in the carnal sense, but the spiritual. My heart leaps with-in to know that I'm a tiny part of an awesome war that will and is taking place. Unlike in the armed forces in the physical, we can't see our enemy.

In the "Gladiator" The enemy actually believes that his formable foe, is dead. The look on his face is priceless when he comes face to face with the one who will take his life and a victory for all of Rome. I serve The Commander in Chief of the Army of the Lord. My loyalty to Him is like the "Gladiator." I plan to fight to the end, knowing that I will someday, get to enjoy the victory that is before me.

The Lord has given me many visions and dreams. Some have already come to pass and others I'm still waiting for. I will be sharing those in the pages to come. I have been called to fight the good fight of faith. I would grossly under estimate my enemy if I thought for one minute my battle was limited to the flesh. Ephesians 6:12 says, "For we do not wrestle against flesh and blood, but against principalities, against the rulers of the darkness of this age, against spiritual hosts of wickedness in the heavenly places."

God doesn't allow us to fight unarmed. In the vision, I was fully dressed for the battle.

Ephesians 6:13-18 states, "Therefore take up the whole armor of God that you may be able to withstand in the evil day, and having done all, to stand. Stand therefore, having girded your waist with truth, having put on the breastplate of righteous, and having shod your feet with the preparation of peace; above all, taking the shield of faith with which you will be able to quench all the fiery darts of the wicked one. And take the helmet of salvation, and the word of God; praying always with all prayer and supplication in the Spirit, being watchful to this end with all perseverance and supplication for all the saints."

The "Gladiator" and I have a lot in common. It doesn't say but, I think whoever wrote that script might have had some insight to the word of God.

A Captive Audience

I PICKED UP A HITCH-HIKER back in 1984 that was obviously tired of walking and was scorched by the blazing Texas sun. He was young, and seemed needy and I never thought anything about pulling over, to let him in to rest his weary legs. Looking back, I'm not sure if I had even asked him where he was headed.

I had a hidden agenda for picking him up. I had just gotten saved, and I was "busting at the seams" to share the gospel with someone, anyone. Never once did it occur to me that this man might have a gun and try to steal my car or try to hurt me. I didn't pre-judge this person except to think that there may just be a slight chance that he was going to go to hell.

If I don't share the gospel, what's the point in getting saved? Jesus was the first fruit of a harvest that will come; I wanted to be a part of that, so it was up to me to do my part. I wanted to share in that harvest.

I was so shocked to find that my new friend had no desire to hear the Word of God. It might have had something to do with the fact that he barely got into the car before I started flooding him information about Jesus. The look on his face seemed to say, "What did I get myself into."

I was bubbling over, and having a captive audience wasn't something I was used to having. He smiled and thanked me for the ride and asked to be let out just up the road a ways. I would have been more than glad to take him where ever it was that he wanted to go in return for a listening ear, after all, the conversations I had through the day was with 2,5 and 7 year olds who really didn't want to talk, at least about what I wanted to talk about.

As he exited the car, I gave him a great big God Bless, and sent him on his way. I was pumped. I started immediately to look for the next person God was going to put in my path. I was soon reprimanded when I shared that story with those who cared about me. They couldn't appreciate the fact that I had picked up a stranger who had been hitch-hiking. I became a little confused since these same people had told me that I needed to trust God in my life. I was a new Christian and didn't know not to provoke God or test Him. I look back on that day now and see the danger I could have been in if, God would have chosen not to protect me, but then, the bible talks about entertaining angels unaware. Maybe that's what I did that day.

Not long after that incident, I received news that my aunt had passed away and that I needed to accompany my dad to Ohio for the funeral. It was a great opportunity for my dad and I to spend a little quality time together and I jumped at the chance. It was the dead of winter and a snow storm had hit back home. We didn't know about the bad weather until we were dropped off at the airport. It was supposed to be a late flight, and the last one leaving that night. (Go figure).

Being the optimist in the family, I resigned myself to believe that God had arranged this and surely something was going to happen. Sitting in front of me was a person that was dressed rather strangely. I was unfamiliar with the Hara Krishna's and didn't realize that's the movement he was a part of until I enthusiastically struck up a conversation with him.

He was very inclined to hear what I had to say. I thanked God that He had given me another opportunity to share the truth. Hours went by; this guy must have had the patience of a saint because all night long, I talked with him about my faith and welcomed him to share his. At one point through the night, I looked over at my dad, who by the way, was not sharing my enthusiasm and was greatly concerned for the poor man that was a prisoner to our conversation. Longsuffering is the word that would describe this gentleman.

I actually got to experience what it means when they say, time fly's." Before I knew it, dad and I were boarding our flight and it was if I had not missed a wink of sleep. I bid my friend good-bye and told him I hope we would meet again someday in heaven.

Since then, my journey with God has been very exhilarating. I have been up hill, down in the valleys, over open plains and in the trenches with Him. I don't regret one day since He has come into my life. When I feel myself getting complacent or far away from Him, He Woo's me back, calling me to commune and take part in the fascinating adventures that await me. I never stray too far and when I think back to all the wondrous times that my life is filled with, I remember the one I adore, for He is my first love.

Mark 16:15 "And he said to them, Go into all the world and preach the gospel to every creature, He who believes and is baptized will be saved; but he who does not believe will be condemned."

Spell Bound

JEWEL T IS A LOW cost grocery store in the Deep South. I never heard of it before I moved to Texas. When I moved there, I was very glad to see that there were places I could afford to shop. I'm not one that has been born with a "silver spoon" in my mouth, so I'm all about being frugal, to the point that my daughter sent me a quote from a book she was reading. It said; "Frugality without creativity is deprivation." She thanked me for all the different ways that I was capable of making something out of nothing and made it fun, so she would never have to know it was because we were poor. She realizes now that she may have to drawl from that same strength.

Cheap grocery stores are not the only thing the south is known for. There are spiritual mediums on every corner. I have always felt uncomfortable when seeing them because of the way I was taught. I got saved in an Assembly of God church and it is taught, and I think rightfully so, that it's forbidden to seek out a medium to glance into your future.

Strangely enough, I was headed to the Jewel T, one steamy hot afternoon. As I pulled into the parking lot of the plaza, I was paralyzed, not of fear, but physically. Not only could I not move my body, I couldn't speak out loud. (It was the fall of the year and Halloween was right around the corner. That's one holiday that I have always refused to celebrate as a Christian.)

In my mind I called out to the Lord and immediately I was able to move. Not understanding what had happened to me, knowing I was not crazy, I began to praise the Lord and pray about what had happened to me. I finished my shopping and got out of there as fast as I could.

Later that afternoon I ran into a Christian friend and began to share with her what I had experienced while at that plaza. Much to my surprise, she had put her application in at the new restaurant that had just opened there. She didn't take the job because it was being run by a spiritual medium that had come up from Mexico. My friend was convinced that the medium was sent there to cast spells on people through the Halloween season. We began to pray against any spirits that could bring harm or that would be used for the benefit of wreaking havoc. Not long after we began to pray, the restaurant was forced to close for lack of business.

I have never before or since experienced anything like that. It showed me that I serve a God who hears my prayers and is stronger than the enemy that wars in the heavens. I hope I never experience anything like that again.

Ephesians 6:12 "For we wrestle not against flesh and blood, but against principalities, against powers, against the rulers of the darkness of this age, against spiritual hosts of wickedness in the heavenly places."

Psalms 46:1 "God is our refuge and strength, a very present help in trouble."

I may have to struggle with the powers of darkness, but I never have to do it alone.

Giving and Receiving

I'm a pretty good judge of character, and when I see people who are happy about giving, it does something in my spirit. An amazing thing happened to me this week; I had the revelation of giving and receiving.

I've always thought of myself as a giver, but I never took into consideration that we are all givers and we are all receivers. We were created to give and receive. I think about the air we breathe. I receive air in to my lungs and give out carbon dioxide. I speak, and the words that I speak out of my mouth are almost always received by someone else. Regardless of whether I want to give or not, I do it without even thinking about it. The person I'm speaking it to, is on the receiving end, whether they want to be or not, and sometimes they don't want to be. If I'm often on the receiving end of things that are hurtful, I am much more likely to turn right around and either spew hurtful things back to the one who is upsetting me, or I end up saying something to someone else that has nothing to do with what is going on, because of my anger.

In Deuteronomy 28, I read about God putting before the children of Israel, curses and blessings and telling them that they get to make the decision of which one they will choose. I do that too, every time I speak a word to someone. I get to decide whether that word will lift someone up or tear them down. I not only pick the cursing or blessing on myself, but I decide whether or not I'm going to pronounce blessing on someone else who has no control over my mouth and at many times are at my mercy with what I speak.

A friend of mine once told me that words are containers of power. I never really understood what that meant until I thought about little children who get yelled at all the time. Their tiny spirits are broken by being on the receiving end of their parent's wrath. I counsel clients who have a very difficult time believing anything good about themselves because they've heard such negative things when they were growing up. We are all participators whether we want to be or not. The question is; what am I giving?

Last week a child came into the facility and it was evident that someone had hit him very hard across the face with their hand. This small child was just 16 months and one of the happiest little people I have ever seen. His face was covered in bruises. I was furious. I made a call to the Child Protective Services and reported this to the person on call. I just wanted to hold him and tell him everything was going to be ok and that I would never allow anything like that to every happen to him again, but couldn't. He will be protected while he is here, but when he leaves we will have no control of what happens to him. This little one doesn't want to be on the receiving end of that abuse.

The bible says that we will give an account for every idle word we speak. I also hope that whoever harmed that child will give an account for what they did. I need to be mindful and make sure the words I speak bring life. I think about some of the words that are used to describe the hurtful things that I have spoken, words that are cruel, spiteful, cutting, wounding, insensitive, inappropriate, tactless, I'm sure the list can go on and on. Now I want to replace them with; pleasant, adorable, exquisite, beautiful, attractive and charming words. Those words are easier on the ears and on the heart.

Psalms 19:14 "Let the words of my mouth and the meditation of my heart be acceptable in your sight, oh Lord, my strength and my Redeemer."

I now ask myself, do the words I speak, bring life or death to the hearer?

Stumbling Oxen

"AGAIN DAVID GATHERED ALL THE choice men of Israel, thirty thousand. And David arose and went with all the people who were with him from Baale Judah to bring up from there the ark of God, whose name is called by the name, the Lord of Hosts, who dwells between the cherubim. So they set the ark of God on a new cart, and brought it out of the house of Abinadab, which was on the hill; and Uzzah and Ahio, the sons of Abinadab, drove the new cart. And they brought it out of the house of Abinadab, which was on the hill, accompanying the ark of God; and Ahio went before the ark. Then David and all the house of Israel played music before the Lord on all kinds of instruments of fir wood, on harps, on stringed instruments, on tambourines, on sistrums, and on cymbals. And when they came to Nachon's threshing floor, Uzzah put out his hand to the ark of God, and took hold of it, for the oxen stumbled. Then the anger of the Lord was aroused against Uzzah, and God struck him there for his error; and he died there by the ark of God." 2 Samuel 6:1-7

I'VE STUDIED THE ARK OF God for a long time. I first read about it in Exodus 24 & 25. The Lord had desired for Moses to come up to the mountain of the Lord and "be there." This speaks volumes to me about the kind of relationship that God is seeking of man. God wanted a place for Him to set a mercy seat. Not just for Moses, but, in time, for, who-so-ever. How awesome for God to love me so much that He would make a place that I could come and receive of His mercy. God desires relationship with man. He wants so much to commune with him, a place to come and be intimate, a place of spiritual intercourse. The Ark would be that place, a place of covenant.

The ark held the Ten Commandments, Arrons budding rod, and manna, (food that God supplied the children of Israel with during their wilderness experience.) Most of all it was the meeting place where the sacred would commune with imperfect man. The Ten Commandments represented the spiritual food that we partake of each time we open and read the Word of God. The budding rod of Aaron, represented the Authority that we walk in as we war against the enemy of our soul. The manna represented the provision that God supplied for forty years in the wilderness when the children of Israel had nothing else to eat. Philippians 4:19 says that "He supplies all our needs according to His riches in Glory in Christ Jesus."

I can only thank God that I live in the age of grace. As I think about how Uzzah's story must have played out, was Uzzah careless? Was he so accustomed to having the ark around that he forgot how holy God was in it? Did he not think before he acted? And where was he the instant God took him. Was it one step over into heaven? I think he probably spiritually slept until Jesus triumphed and went into hell immediately following His crucifixion. (But that's another story, Ephesians 4:9)

I cringe to think how many times I could have been struck dead because of the mistakes I've made in my life. I'm thankful that because of what Jesus did at Calvary; my mistakes have all been paid for. When I received all He had done for me by asking Jesus into my heart, I believe no matter if I was to be struck dead today, I would go to heaven.

I have a lot of questions to ask when I go to Heaven. Not just for God but also for Uzzah, because I think he's there. Questions like, what were you thinking? If you could go back and relive that moment, what would you do differently? Or maybe I would ask, have you ever eaten the almonds from Aaron's budding rod?

Here's another thought, suppose that Uzzah took on some false responsibility. We know that man had already put the Ark on the cart, which was man's way of doing things. The Ark was to be carried on the shoulders of the priests. God didn't need Uzzah to save the ark that day. Often we take on the responsibility for the things that we shouldn't. I think it says to God that He is not able to do things without our help and if we don't do the things that we think absolutely has to get done, that things will fall apart.

What if, there's no praise and worship team to stand in front of the congregation and sing? What if there is no piano player to play for the people that shows up to worship the Lord? I think God will show up no matter who else does, and if that happens with or without a piano player, it will be the best time with the Lord that we have ever experienced.

I stayed for Sunday school one time when there were just four of us and the Sunday school teacher didn't even stay. We had the best time. The Holy Spirit showed up and I could sense Him moving all over me. I could hardly stand up. I sat there thinking how awesome it was that God didn't depend on a lot of people in order for Him to move. Matthew 18:20 says "where there are two or three gathered together, He is in the midst." If we linger in His presence, and don't get in a hurry to leave, God will show up and when He does, there will always be something awesome take place.

Romans 6:23 "For the wages of sin is death, but the gift of God is eternal life in Christ Jesus our Lord." God has order and those who follow Him will need to follow that order.

Juanita and the Tiny Yellow Peeps

THE ENVELOPE WAS DELIVERED WITH 3 teeny holes. The picture of rushing water, over jagged rocks, in a fairly large creek still remained. There was a short letter describing the items inside, but without knowing what the missing pieces were, she had no way of knowing exactly what the author of the letter was trying to tell her. The letter was anonymous because it came from Juanita's pen pal.

I received a call from the recipient of the letter who was excited that she had received the letter, but was frustrated that half of the message was missing. She knew by the description of the paralleling theme that it was going to be quite interesting when she cracked the unsolved mystery.

It was all I could do to keep quiet and let her speak. I couldn't have planned this any better if I had tried. I hadn't intended for the little peeps to work their way through the envelope before they had arrived at their final destination. I was however pleased to know that she was so blessed by the letter that explained the picture and what it stood for. I wrote about how life can be rocky at times and how no matter what we were going through the Lord would always be there to see us through. I quoted scripture about how God doesn't always keep us from things but always goes with us through the hard times.

She had no idea that I was her secret pal. Weeks went by and the missing peeps kept her in suspense. Finally, the night came when our secret pal was to be revealed. This night was going to be extra special for Juanita, because she had been waiting with great expectation. We ate the dinner and one by one each person shared what their secret pal had done for them throughout the previous months. I was sitting by Juanita when she began to share her experiences of the different ways her secret pal had blessed her.

Much to my surprise I won the prize for the most unique gift that was given. We had the best time talking about those months, when she found out that I was her secret pal. That was a bonding moment for us. It was then that I was able to explain the little peeps and I had sent her in the mail. Jesus, in Matthew 23 spoke these words; "Jerusalem, Jerusalem, the one who kills the prophets and stones those who are sent to her! How often I wanted to gather your children together, as a hen gathers her chicks under her wings, but you were not willing". I wanted her to know that Jesus always wants to gather us together and will, at some point in this life, so that we can all be together.

We grew closer and closer , and she became like a spiritual mother to me. I knew nothing of the word, and was struggling daily to walk accordingly. I had a desire and I now know that God honored that. Juanita allowed me to call her day or night if I needed to.

Years have come and gone, Juanita and I have been through the good, bad and the ugly together. Whenever one of us is in need of a shoulder to cry on, we are there for each other. I haven't made many friends in this life, but when I found her I found a real jewel. We live 1200 miles away from each other. I have moved, like a gypsy back and forth from Ohio to Texas, over the last 30 years. That has not stopped us from growing closer and closer to each other.

I teach my clients to look for sponsors while they are in the program of recovery. If they are fortunate to find someone who is half the friend and accountability partner that Juanita has been to me, they are truly blessed.

John 15:13 "Greater love has no one than this, than to lay down one's life for his friends." I truly think that she has been such a good friend to me, that it wouldn't take much to convince me to lay my life down for her.

Entertaining Angels Unaware

BLOOD RAN DOWN THE SIDE of my head as I tried to pull myself loose from between my car and the 18 wheeler that had crashed into me as I attempted to make a left hand turn. I felt the sting of the accident and realized that I was the closest to death that I had ever been. My spirit felt like it was trying to break free from my body and the thought ran through my mind that this may be what it feels like to have an out of the body experience. I was having difficulty breathing, and felt that there had been damage to my lungs. It felt as if my lung was punctured. I found out later I had broken my ribs.

My sister Glenda and my aunt Myrt was with me. We were on our way to have lunch with my husband. I had seen his truck at a parts store, as we were driving by and when I made the left hand turn to cross the highway, the truck came up behind me and hit into the left side of my car crushing it beyond recognition. The on-coming traffic saw everything that happened and was able to give a statement in my behalf. Had the truck driver decided to miss me she would have hit the on-coming car head-on and someone would have probably been killed.

My husband told one of the men that were helping us that he was going to go direct traffic because "whoever is in that vehicle is more than likely dead". He had no idea that it was his wife and family. When they told him it was me in the car he freaked out.

We were transported by an e-squad to a hospital in Palestine, Texas. I had been seen by a Dr. Smith. I had asked someone there what his name was. He had told me in the Er. I had fractured my ribs, had a two inch cut on my head, my leg had tissue damage done to it, the ulnar nerve in my left arm was smashed, I had two discs in my back that was damaged, and that someone had already got to me before I got to the hospital. I was alive and very grateful that God was not ready for me yet.

My sister sustained injuries in her mouth and fractured her collar bone. My aunt was pretty beat up with cuts and bruises and we were thankful that it wasn't a lot worse. When she arrived home from the airport my uncle was shocked at the sight of her. I had to go back to the hospital a month later and have surgery on the ulnar nerve in order to get the motor skills and feeling back into my fingers. I have yet to see the manifestation of the healing in my fingers. The Lord had healed everything else.

Several months had gone by and I kept wondering why I had not received a bill from the doctor who treated me. I had received many other bills from the hospital, but his was not one of them. I finally called and ask for the billing department and ask why I had not received a bill from Dr. Smith. They informed me that there was no Dr. Smith that worked there and they would check to see if a Dr. Smith had been brought in from another hospital working on call that day. Once they checked it out, they confirmed that there had been no such Doctor there and was I sure I had the right hospital. I thanked them for their time and hung up the phone. I have yet to get a bill for the services rendered by Dr. Smith or any other Doctor that day. I can't explain it, but I know the one who can.

Hebrews 13:2" Do not forget to entertain strangers, for by so doing some has unwittingly entertained angels."

Caution

THE YELLOW RIBBON WAS ROPED from one end of the trailer to the other. I could see my mother's belongings thrown here and there. My sisters, brother and I were told that we could not cross the yellow tape. It was an eerie feeling, more like a dream than anything else. Back then the T.V. shows like CSI and Cold Case hadn't come out yet, but there were shows like; Dragnet, Perry Mason and Hawaii Five O. All of which had the same tape that kept people from crossing over and touching things they weren't supposed to.

My mother had been shot and killed in a bar. I'm thinking the tape was there too, but I can't remember, because I lived so far away and by the time I reached the crime scene, everything had already been taken care of. To be honest I was in shock, so I can't really remember. I do how ever remember the tape at my mother's trailer and I thought it rather rude of whoever had put it there. We didn't stay at the trailer long, just enough time to get her personal belongings. We found out that because my step father lived long enough to get to the hospital that everything they owned , now belonged to his family. It didn't seem to matter that he took her life and to me that should have been enough for us to be able to have some of their belongings. The surviving family members did agree to pay for her funeral arrangements, but even that came with a price, for we had to have her in the same room as he was in for the showing.

Ever since my mother's death, when I see the word, "caution" that's what I think about. I also think about the way I feel when I know that I need to tread lightly in situations that may put me in harm's way, for instance when I'm working with a client who has come to our facility who has previously been incarcerated for a domestic violence charge. The last thing that I want to do is provoke the client. I see that clearly and know not to go there, but there are others who don't seem to get that.

Some of the client's that I work with love to needle people and single their peers out if they don't particularly like them. I truly don't think that they have the understanding of what is capable of happening as a result of bulling someone who has dealt with those issues.

When the spirit of murder is not renounced in a person's life after they have committed that crime, I believe it opens the door for that person to be able to kill again. Look at serial killers, It appears to be easier each time they kill again and again.

My heart goes out to the client's that have been abused to the point that they don't care what they have to face to be able to end the life of devastation that they have faced at the hands of their abuser. The idea of prison probably doesn't see so bad after what they've been through. Regardless of why people choose to kill, justified or not, doesn't remove them from the consequences of spirits that can take over a person's life because of a sin that has been committed such as murder. It's my opinion of course, but without renouncing and asking forgiveness, I think the person sets himself or herself up to kill again or at the very least continues to deal with the aftermath of anger and frustration that is built up and if never dealt with, that person can be a walking time bomb.

A lot of clients I see have hate issues. I want to hold them and tell them that if they could just give God a chance in their lives, that He alone can heal them from the hurt that they have faced. I can't answer the question of why God would allow the abuse to have happened in the first place, in fact that's probably one of the first things that I want to ask Him when I get to heaven. For now though, I do know that He is able to put His hand on our heart and keep us from feeling the pain that haunts us every day. I know this, because I myself have been sexually molested and raped.

I have felt the pain and I have experienced the healing. It doesn't have to rule my life, I won't allow it. It was enough that they were able to still that innocence from me, I can't allow them to have anymore of me. They will answer for what they did someday.

The hate that I felt from being abused could have ended in me taking a life or too myself. So I get it. I know the eruption of hate that can explode from your being. I also know the freedom from the pain that I've experienced since that day that I forgave them for what they did. I also had to forgive my step father for killing my mother. He rarely takes up space in my head. I have the hope that I will see my mother again. I may also see him and if I do, I can honestly say that I will be able to feel nothing of the hate and anger that once ruled my life.

I see the potential of what hate can do. I feel it when I walk in the room of a client who is provoked. I deeply respect the one with the anger and I want them to be set free. I still to this day feel the "caution" and I see the tape in my mind's eye. I'm free, that's my choice!

Romans 12:19 " Beloved, do not avenge yourselves, but rather give place to wrath; for it is written, Vengeance is Mine, I will repay, says the Lord."

The Scarlet Rope of Hope

SHE WORE HER FOUR INCH red satin heels, a pair of pretty black shorts and a red backless strapped blouse for the sick perverted men, she knew would be cruising the strip. As evening fell, The Seven-Eleven parking- lot, in Wheeling West Virginia, began to fill up with pimps, prostitutes, and the homeless.

It was hard to make the kind of money that she used to make in Las Vegas but it wasn't because she didn't try. She was a beautiful, thin, strong-headed female, who loved to flaunt what she had and knew she could make a lot of money with little effort. It made it very difficult to want to get a job that would make an honest living. It was sad because of the potential I knew she had. Her dream was to go back to school and regain custody of her children who she loved very much.

Dreams are often shattered when the power of addiction is stronger than the ability to stay clean. Needs are difficult to meet when all you know is to sell yourself to the highest bidder. It wouldn't have been out of her reach to become a doctor or a lawyer's wife, but something must have happened a long time ago to take her down the path that she had chosen. I hope that someday she will seize an opportunity to make something out of herself.

The bible tells a story of a prostitute that did just that. Rahab realized that God had given the land she lived in, to the children of Israel. The day would soon come when she and her family would be killed if she didn't do something. The spies were there to seek out the land and overtake and occupy it. The orders would be for them to kill everyone, women and children included.

Rahab knew that she had nothing to lose by making a deal with those who held her life in their hands. She hid the spies from those who sought them out. She lied to the king's men and told them that the spies had been there and told the soldiers where to look for them. Rahab told the spies that she knew the Lord had given them the land and that terror had fallen on the city. Everyone had heard how the Lord had parted the Red Sea and let the children of Israel pass over on dry land.

Rahab begged for her life. Knowing that she had showed them kindness, the men were more than willing to bargain with her. They spoke words of life to her when they said, "Our lives for yours if none of you tell this business of ours. And it shall be, when the Lord has given us the land that we will deal kindly and truly with you." The men sealed the deal with a sign, "We will be blameless of this oath of yours which you have made us swear, "unless, when we come into the land, you bind this line of scarlet cord in the window through which you let us down, and unless you bring your father, your mother, your brothers, and all your fathers household to your own home. So shall it be that whoever goes outside the doors of your house, his blood shall be on his own head, and we will be guiltless. Joshua 2.

The men held true to their word and Rahab and her family were kept safe. Rahab's life was changed from that very day. The book of Matthew gives an account of the Genealogy of Jesus and in the 5th verse of the 1st chapter you can find Rahab's name. God not only spared her live, but made it possible to be counted among the blood line of the Savior of the world. God always goes beyond our wildest imagination, when He chooses to bless us. The awesome thing about God, He is no respecter of persons. What God did for Rahab, He will do for that prostitute in Wheeling, West Virginia!

The Prophetess

SHE TOWERED ABOVE THE CROWD and her presence commanded your attention. Not because it had anything to do with her, but because she was hidden in the presence of the Lord. The word of God say's that God doesn't share His glory with another and even though I knew she wasn't coveting His glory, it appeared to engulf her.

She spoke with the authority that God has given us as His children. She ministered with all she had in her and it was causing her to be weary. I'm not sure how many days she had been ministering but I knew this was not the first night that she had been there.

She didn't know my name, so she called to me by describing the color of my shirt and pointing in my direction. I stumbled to the front of the church because I am not very graceful on my feet. I stood in front of her as she stared me in the eye and began to speak things over me that the Lord had already began in me, but that she wasn't aware of.

She told me that I was like "the woman in the well-known picture, of the woman reaping a harvest; they sell at all the Bible book stores." But she said I "wasn't reaping a harvest, I was actually sowing seed and that I did it continually for the Lord." She told me that "God going to begin to stir with-in me a gift of wisdom and that I would need to sit at the feet of God and search His heart to see how to sow the word of God into the lives of those I would be meeting where God was taking me."

She said that "God was going to give me clarity of the Word and that I was not to get prideful or haughty using the gift that God was giving me. I was to give it with purity and with compassion and mercy and that when it was given in this manner the seed would be planted deep. She also said that I would not be aware of the results of the seeds that were sowed in those I was sowing, but that down the road I would know of the fruit."

I knew exactly what she meant. I had already been sowing and God had already been giving me clarity of the Word. The one thing I was concerned about was that I was to search God's heart and sit at His feet. I can sit at His feet, but how do you search God's heart? It must be humongous. Where would I start? I knew doors were being opened and things were going to be, "exceedingly, abundantly above anything that I could ever dream of." Searching the Father's heart was going to be a journey in itself. I could tell already this was going to be wonderful.

You never serve God without paying the price. The prophetess knew this from the various hardships that she has been through. While she was ministering to us, the enemy was wreaking havoc at her house. This isn't just any house it is God's House. It is a house that has been built for orphans who have nowhere to go. God's Word says that this is perfect religion; when people care for the widows and orphans. The devil didn't want her telling us the things she spoke. I was blessed to see that she immediately gave it over to God and continued to do His work.

I went the following Sunday night to hear her speak again and took my dear friend, sister and partner with me. She also received a word that night. I would need her permission to share so I will just say that it was right on the mark.

That night the prophetess told us to "go home and wrestle with the word that we had been given and not let if fall by the way side." I did just that and as I gave myself to the Father and began trying to figure out how to search His heart in order to receive the wisdom I knew I would need for the road ahead, I wasn't disappointed with the time I spent with Him.

I began to weep as I was given a revelation of the word that I had received. I opened my bible to Mark 4 and began reading about the sower that went out to sow. I was realizing for the first time that the ground in which I had sowed had not been properly prepared. When I thought about all the times that I witnessed to others and had even lead many to the Lord, I thought about the fruit that had come from that time of sowing and realized that it had not been near as fruitful as it would have been had I just prepared the ground a little better before I planted the seed.

It made me sick to think that I would probably not get a second chance to work in those fields, so I immediately prayed to the Father that He would sent laborers into those fields and have them cultivate the ground and sow into those fields deeper than I was able to sow. I didn't feel condemned, for I didn't have the revelation of that word until now. As I prayed the word, I knew the Father, in the name of Jesus would sent laborers and I would hear at another time of those fields producing the kind of fruit I wanted them to produce. I was very thankful for the opportunity to see a great harvest, all because I took the time to sit at the Father's feet and allow Him to stir the gift of wisdom in me that the prophetess said the Father would stir. God is faithful. He wants His children to know things. I know it is the Fathers good pleasure to show us the mystery of the Kingdom.

It's no coincidence that my business partner and I are about to begin spiritual warfare boot camps all over the nation. God does not send us out unequipped. "He supplies all our needs according to His riches in glory." Phil. 4:19. I needed this information so that I can cultivate and prepare the ground for the seed I am going to be sowing.

The end of the story will have to come in the next book I write. I stand in faith and I know that awesome things are going to happen. My greatest desire is to bring Glory to His name. I have given my notice at work that by the end of the year I will be going into full time ministry. I will no longer work in the field of drug and alcohol treatment.

I'm turning over a new leaf. It's a Hugh leap of faith but I serve a big God and I know that "He is able to keep that which I had committed unto Him against that day." (2 Tim. 1:12).

Prophesy is a beautiful thing when you know that it comes from the Lord. In the field of addiction we too often see self-fulfilling prophesy from client's who see nothing good in themselves. They speak harm over themselves all the time. The words come out of their mouths and they never think a thing about it. I'm glad that I have a Father in Heaven that believes in me and wants nothing but my best and sees to it that I get it. I am truly blessed.

People sometimes get freaked out when the conversation comes up about spiritual issues such as prophesy or speaking in tongues or different kinds of spiritual gifts, but if you can line everything up with the word of God then I think it is a safe thing to trust in, as long as we "try every spirit." (1John 4:1.)

Twilight

THERE IS A PLACE BETWEEN darkness and light were we are fighting. It's not a place where vampires chase each other and try to suck your blood to live another day. It is a place where real war is being fought between the flesh and the spirit. It's a place where I'm put at times when the Lord is trying to do a work in me.

It was just recently brought to my attention that there were some things in me that make me very UN appealing. I had been blinded to what it was until I was shown by the Lord so I could change it. I had it so that I would be ineffective. There is a passage in the bible that talks about the enemy coming at night and sowing tares into a field where someone had taken great care to prepare a ground that would produce a plentiful harvest. (Matt. 13:24-30).

Because the enemy wants to destroy any good thing that we do, he will plant bad in the good that we try to produce. It wasn't able to be dealt with in me until I started a fast for an event that was coming up that I knew would be effective. I have always fasted in the past, hoping God would bring about changes in others, things like salvation and deliverance. What I hadn't seen until now is that the fast that I had chosen actually worked to take the blinders off me so that I would be humbled enough to be willing to be stripped from the dross that made me unclean. In the night hours I woke tossing and turning because I was acutely aware that I was going to have a struggle with what to wear to work. This was a strange thing for me to be thinking about in the midst of all that was going on in my life.

There was a disappointment in me as I remembered the previously night and how God had woke me up with the thoughts of the spiritual warfare boot camp and the things I was to speak about it. The thought of me having trouble with what to wear just didn't seem to fit, (pardon the pun.) The Lord had reminded me of a conversation I had earlier that day about a previous client that I had a hard time relating to. I had said some unkind things, not about her but about me not wanting to be there if she was going to return for a stay. It was not pretty. All of a sudden I realized what a terrible person I was and had been all my live. The only difference between me and her was that I had received the gift that God have given me at the Cross by giving His only begotten Son. All the thoughts of my struggle finally made sense. I was between the darkness and the light and I was fighting. I had on cloths of self-righteousness and they were as filthy rags in the sight of God. The turmoil wasn't for what I was to wear in the natural but it was a fight for what I was to wear in the spiritual. How could I fit into my self-righteous rags when God had given me a robe of righteousness that Jesus had gone to the Cross to purchase on my behalf?

It was no coincidence that what I was to teach on that next weekend was the armor that we are to wear when we do spiritual warfare. No wonder God had to deal with my heart. The pride and haughtiness that God was dealing with me about for the last couple weeks was right there in front of my eyes.

The enemy had sown seeds of judgmental thoughts into my life and then blinded me so I could not be effective in the work that God was preparing me to do. Now, the Lord is faithful if we will heed to His word and if we will be obedient to the things that He calls us to do. Had I not fasted as instructed by the Lord I might not had been able to see the self-righteous rags that needed to be stripped from me. I repented, and ask God to keep dealing with me until all that was not right in me was gone.

It's hard to accept the things in us that are less than pleasant. God had warned me earlier that pride and haughtiness could be an issue and that I was to sit at the Lords feet and ask for wisdom for the word that was coming forth in me. I had no idea that it would be a word for me first. If that word had come from anyone else I would probably not have been able to receive it.

There's a lot to be said for self- reflection. I am a work in progress and the Lord will be working on me until the day He returns for His bride. I can't afford to be arrogant and puffed up, nor do I want to be. I prayed for God to extract anything from me that would be detrimental to Him and the work that needs to be done. That can be painful, but that's the price you pay if the work is to come through the fire refined.

I love people and I know that God sees us all the same in His eyes. "He died for each one of us while we were yet sinners." (Romans 5:8).

God wasn't through with talking to me that night; He had some other things that He wanted me to stop doing. I had been angry with the company that I was working for and was withholding a blessing from them that I knew He wanted me to bless them with. I had some material that I had been using in my groups that I had created and that no-one else had access to. One of the therapists had offered to buy it from me because I was leaving the company and they wanted to be able to use my work to continue the groups as I had taught them. Because of my anger issues, I didn't want to sell them my work and was acting like a spoiled child determined not to let them benefit from anything I had created.

My eyes were opened to the fact that God was less than pleased with me for my behavior and I knew in my heart that though I was unwilling to sell the company my material, I would now be giving it to them free of charge. I was not accountable for the way the company had been treating me but I was accountable for the way that I was treating them. I knew that if I was disobedient I would regret it in the end. Nothing is worth blocking what God wants to do in my life. God and I go back a long way and I know when I am disobedient, that it delays the work that I am called to do. God has always been gentle with me. He will wait for me to learn the lessons I need to learn. It doesn't take as long as it used to. Like I said, I'm a work in progress.

I didn't get much sleep that night, but what I did receive was vital for the work of the kingdom. I don't mind missing out on sleep when I'm wrestling with my Father. The neat thing about that is; He is able to give me rest in my spirit and I don't have to feel tired because He is able to give me supernatural strength to make it through the day. As for what to wear to work, the important thing was that I knew what not to wear!

Blessed

PRAY FOR YOUR ENEMIES. I never understood how that was possible. Why would I want to bless those who hated me, hurt me, and took advantage of me? Was there something I wasn't seeing? I knew the scriptures say that Gods ways are not our ways, and that Gods thoughts are not our thoughts. That His ways are higher than our ways, but I just didn't get it. Oh I do now, but it took praying about it and stepping out in faith to see it.

I guess I really got it one day when I was praying for my grandchildren. My granddaughter's mother was seeing someone who wasn't a very kind person and he always took it out on my granddaughter. My heart would break, when my sweet little granddaughter would come to me and tell me how she was being treated by him. My first thought was to rip his head off and ask questions later. My anger was really blinding me of the answer. I could get angry and fight with this guy, but it wasn't going to solve anything, and it was only going to make matters worse for my granddaughter.

The answer was to pray blessings on this guy. I know that sounds like I have lost my mind, but I know that's what Jesus would do. As I began to pray for him, my heart didn't seem to be so heavy. I then began getting reports of this guy not coming around so much. I really did want God to bless him and when I prayed for him it seemed that God wasn't just blessing him, He was also blessing me. I was planting seeds of blessing in this guy's life and I was reaping a harvest. I wasn't the only one reaping a harvest, so was my granddaughter.

The key to being able to appreciate the concept of blessing those that make your life miserable is that when God begins to bless them, they change because the blessings in their life keep them from being so miserable and it keeps them from making others miserable too.

The blessings that you pronounce on them aren't always material things, but things that cause them to change and get right. A blessed person may be blessed with being able to make good decisions, or make moral decisions that make them do the right thing. If they do the right thing, they won't be so quick to do bad things to good people.

I prayed a blessing on a client one time that was making my life miserable. She got picked up the very next weekend for driving under the influence. Now you might say how is that a blessing for her? Well she didn't kill someone while under the wheel driving, and she didn't kill herself while driving, so It was a blessing that she got picked up without anyone getting hurt. It also gave her the opportunity to get some help before something really bad happened. If I would have had the attitude that kept me from praying for her, something else might have happened.

When we think of blessing someone, we need to remember that there will be changes in that person's life that can make things better for other people. Why wouldn't I want to speak blessings over them?

This concept was such an awesome revelation to me. It is causing me to speak blessings over people I don't even know. Where I used to have road rage, now I have peace. When I use to be full of anxiety, now I'm calm. It has made my days so much better that I can't wait for an opportunity to bless people, so I can see the different ways God will work in their lives.

So what's the alternative? Let's take murder for instance. Wow! Where did that come from. I'm not talking about physically taking someone's life, but the Bible say's in (Matthew 5:22) that, " murder begins in the heart." "You have heard it said to those of old, You shall not murder, and who ever murders will be in danger of the judgment.' But I say to you that whoever is angry with his brother without a cause, (road rage) shall be in danger of the judgment."

I think it's better to bless someone and have a harvest of blessings in return, as opposed to having to worry about answering to God about the hate I have in my heart.

The Bible also says, "Give, and it will be given to you: good measure, pressed down, shaken together, and running over will be put into your bosom, For with the same measure that you use, it will be measured back to you."(Luke 6:38) So, if I'm going to be receiving in that way, I really want to be giving a blessing and not a curse, especially if I'm going to get it given back to me in abundance.

"Blessed is he who blesses you, And cursed is he that curses you." (Numbers 24:9).

The Un-returnable Gift

I HAVE ALWAYS WONDERED WHY the devil has been so successful at being destructive. If I was God I would have stripped Satan of every gift God gave to him when he was kicked out of Heaven. Isaiah 14:12 says, "How have you fallen from Heaven, O Lucifer, son of the morning!"

God didn't take away the gifts that He had given Lucifer. That's why he has been so successful at being able to twist things and use them for his own sick intentions.

In Ezekiel 28:13-15 it says, "You were in Eden, the garden of God; every precious stone was your covering: The sardius, topaz, and diamond, Beryl, onyx, and jasper, Sapphire, turquoise, and emerald with gold. The workmanship of your timbrels and pipes was prepared for you on the day you were created. You were the anointed cherub who covers: I established you; you were on the holy mountain of God; you walked back and forth in the midst of fiery stones. You were perfect in your ways from the day you were created, till iniquity was found in you."

That description sounds breath taking. Lucifer had fallen and everything he possessed went with him. He uses what God had given him to lure us away from God because he knows his time is short. He even had the nerve to try to use the word of God against Jesus when Jesus was led away into the wilderness for forty days. (Mark 1:12).

Satan knows the word better than most Christians do. He also knows whether we know the word or not. He took advantage of Eve in the garden because she miss-quoted what God had commanded her to not do. Since Lucifer has fallen he "walks around like a roaring lion seeking whom he may devour". (1st peter 5:8). He can only do that because of the gifts that the Lord has blessed him with before the fall. He twists the word of God to try to mess us up. He is not the only one that does that.

I was thinking about how we can use the things that God gives us to destroy ourselves and others if we are not careful. We can take the word of God and destroy our sisters and brothers if they don't know the word. We can twist it for our own benefit. I think of some of the T.V. preachers who take the word and turn it into a way to become rich. They use the gifts that they have been given and use them to make people believe that they are supposed to give everything they have for the benefit of their ministry.

Some of these poor people don't have enough to live on and yet they are supporting ministers who should be supporting them. Somehow the enemy has been able to infiltrate the camp of the living God and pull the wool right over the eyes of the saved even taking the basic needs and using them to destroy.

I remember hearing a few years back about a girl who entered a contest on the radio where she had to drink a lot of water and hold it for as long as she could. This girl went home and was feeling really bad. That night she died, because of the water she had consumed and the way it affected her kidneys. It blows my mind that you can take something that we use for a basic need and end our lives with it.

God didn't intend for us to use water for a contest to see how much our bodies can hold, but we seem as humans to push the envelope in everything we do. I doubt if that girl knew the danger she was in. I hope she was saved.

The enemy isn't particular what he uses as long as he can destroy us. I think the one thing that makes him most successful is the words of our own mouth. James 3:8 says, " No man can tame the tongue. It is an unruly evil, full of deadly poison." I know that if I'm not careful I can destroy someone with my mouth and justify what I say at the same time. I also know that I will be accountable to God for it when I do and believe me I don't want to go there.

These days I'm very careful what comes from my mouth. James goes on to say in verse 10 that, "out of the same mouth proceed blessing and curses. My brethren, these things ought not to be so." verse 11 and 12, "Does a spring send forth fresh water and bitter from the same opening? Can a fig tree, my brethren, bear olives, or a grapevine bear figs? Thus no spring yields both salt water and fresh."

Father, Put a watch before my mouth that I will praise you and not curse others. I don't want to be like the devil, whose agenda is to "kill, steal and destroy." I want to be someone who will build up and not tear down. Someone who will plant a lush garden free from the tares of the world. A person who will speak life and not death for your word says that, " death and life are in the power of the tongue and those who love it will eat its fruit."(Proverbs 18:21).

God is very careful not to entrust to us, those things that we will use for own agenda. He has waited for years to trust me with things that He knew that I would not know what to do with. I'm thankful that I'm beginning to see that He trusts me with things that I can use in the ministry that will bring glory to His name.

He has been working on me to extract pride, haughtiness and impurities from me that could do harm to the body of Christ. I'm thankful to be rid of those things. The word says, that "God disciplines those He loves". He must love me a lot. I just hope that by the time I get to Heaven that there will be something left. My friend once said that by the time she gets to Heaven, she will be the size of a bb. I guess that's the pruning process.

God gives us gifts, I know it must greatly disappoint Him when we use it for our own benefit. Because they are gifts, His doesn't take them back, even when they are given to who is now His arch enemy.

Truth in a Very Unusual Form

TRUTH COMES IN DIFFERENT FORMS. For me sometimes it comes in the form of a vision. I remember my first vision and I don't completely understand why I was seeing it when I did, but now I know that it was for the days ahead of me. I was standing in a field and it began to rain. It wasn't raining water, it was raining what appeared to be kernels of wheat. I thought it was a strange thing to be coming out of the sky. I held out my hands to retrieve as much of the substance as I could and it didn't take long for my hands to fill up.

I looked around me and the ground was covered and filling with this unusual element. I was alone in the field, so I wasn't able to share it with anyone but I had the distinct impression that I was supposed to give this wealth to others.

I let all that was in my hands fall to the ground so that I could open up one of the grains to see what it possessed. When I broke it open I could see a whole harvest field full of truth. I was overwhelmed by how one small kernel could hold so much information. I was very aware that when this tiny seed was planted that it would produce a hundred fold return. As I looked around, I couldn't imagine how all of it could be planted and harvested. Then I remember thinking about the scripture that said "if all the books that could be written about the Lord would be written, that the world could not hold them all."(John 21:25). Then with that information, I was able at some small level to begin to put it all into perspective, and it didn't hurt to know that "with God all things are possible". (Matt. 19:26).

When the vision was over, I had a desire to plant those seeds, especially because it was truth that I would be planting. Something in me drove me to start planting, without even realizing what I was doing. I fell in love with God's Word so much that it just became a part of me.

I have thought about that vision many times but never understood why

I had it or what I was to do with it. I waited patiently on the Lord for years to reveal it to me, and a couple of weeks ago I finally got it. I wrote a few pages back about a prophetess who spoke over me that I was a planter of seeds for the Lord and that I had done it on a continual basis. The reality of that vision came rushing back to me. I had been trying all these years to plant the seeds that the Lord had showed me in that vision. It was coming to pass on a recurring basis every day that I had shared the Word. I love that vision and it's exciting to me to see it as though it was given to me yesterday. I have visions quite regular, some I have the interpretations for and some I don't.

The first one I had ever received was in Dawson, Texas when I was a fairly new Christian. I was attending a Baptist church there and was so excited to share it with the congregation, that I went to my pastor and ask permission to extend it to my fellow sisters and brothers in Christ. He was not thrilled to have me do so and I was quite surprised that he didn't share in my enthusiasm. It wasn't because he didn't believe it was from the Lord, because he actually did think it was. The reason he wasn't thrilled for me to share, was that he knew they wouldn't accept what I had to say.

He was wise and knew immediately the interpretation of the vision and it was a hard word for the people to receive. I was not aware of the problems in the church, and as I said before, I was new and still in the honeymoon stages of my salvation. I was on fire and thought that every Christian under the sun was too. (Boy, did I get a rude awakening.)

The look on my face must have been priceless when the pastor agreed to let me spill from my lips the oracles of God in my heart. At this point he might have thought, "What have I got to lose." (I found out later that they were trying to get rid of him. It would be their loss because I knew in my heart that this was a true man of God.)

I came the following Sunday and stood to my feet to announce that God had given me a vision and I wanted to reveal to them what it was that the Lord had shared with me. Now, remember, I was greener than a leaf on an old oak tree at the start of spring.

"I see a small child standing outside a tiny white church, dressed for the cold. He wanted so badly to eat some of the fresh snow that had gingerly floated to the ground. He saw that the snow had been tainted with soot and He tried to brush away the impurities so that He could taste of the cold fresh snowfall that appealed to Him. The deeper He dug, the more He realized that the snow was so infiltrated with the soot that it was impossible for Him to partake without eating of its impurities.

The Lord had given me the interpretation of the vision and it was as follows: The tiny child was Jesus wanting to have communion with His children in the church. The soot was coming from with-in the church, representing the people there who had un-forgiven sin in their lives and was refusing to repent. The Lord was wanting to find purity in His children but could not find it.

As I was trying to give the interpretation, a woman was behind me, hitting the pew with her foot so loud that it was hard to speak without feeling distracted. As I turned to see who the lady was making such a racket, I was shocked to see that it was my neighbor from across the street. My heart sank to think that this lady would be so rude to do what she had done.

Later I found out that the people of that church was trying to starve out the pastor and his family. Looking back now I don't doubt that Ichabod has been written across the front door. That word means that "the glory of the Lord has departed."(1Sam.4:21.)

I could see the truth in what the Lord was trying to get across to His children, but they would not accept it. I left the church a few months later. I often wonder what happened to that pastor. I pray in the name of Jesus that he is in a good place. He blessed me while I was there and I truly think he is a good Shepard.

I thought about why that church was lacking so. Then I remembered them always complaining about everything. I never heard anything positive coming out of their mouth. It makes me think of the children of Israel and how they were always murmuring and complaining, even when the Lord did miracle after miracle in their midst. How many times would they have to take another trip around the mountain?

God knows everything. He knew that the children of Israel would get fed up with the wilderness conditions pretty quick, so when He had them leave Egypt, He took them and moved them into the wilderness. (Exodus 13:17).

In spite of the fact that God gave the children of Israel all the provisions they would ever need, including direction by His own cloud and fire, they still cried out in fear, (Exodus 14:10) the kind of fear that broke the Lord's heart. That kind of fear is the lack of faith. I don't say that, without knowing that they didn't have the bible to tell them all the things that we are told, so I get it, but I also know that He was with them and had showed them many times how He could and did save them.

All through-out the book of Exodus, I see the children constantly complaining. I also see God telling Moses to step aside because He was going to destroy them for their lack of faith. What more could they have wanted? He gave them manna and quail when they were hungry. He gave them fire at night to keep them warm in the freezing dessert. He gave them water from a rock. He protected them and fought their battles for them. What He didn't let them do, is cross over into the promise land because of their murmuring and their complaining. Moses, who stood in the gap for them many times, was told that he would not be going over to the other side. He got to see it but he was not able to enter. (Deut.34:1-7).

In the commentary of my Spirit Filled Life Bible it tells me that "in Hebrew thought to see it with your eyes was a symbol of acquisition by which property became legally that of the viewer." So even though Moses didn't get to enter in, he was able to see the land that God promised and he knew that he owned that land because it was given to Abraham and his descendants. (Gen. 13:14,15). "Thus, Moses was accepting, from God ownership of the Promised Land on behalf of all Israel". That's just like God to have such compassion and mercy that He would let Moses see with his eyes the promises He made to Moses ancestors.

I continue to get visions, but I am more careful of when and if I share them. I've learned that even if God performs miracles in the sight of men, that it's no guarantee that they will walk in blind obedience to Him. We all have a choice. We can choose to belief and life will be a grand adventure, or we can murmur and complain like the children or Israel and the people of a pessimistic church and experience life on life's terms. I choose the grand adventure.

The Vehicle of Wisdom

Just recently I was at an altar with our Saturday morning prayer group when the Lord began to give me a vision. We had been asking God for a lot of specific things for our church body and we were not seeing results as we thought we should. It was really weighing on our pastor that we had not seen the type of growth in our church that we believed God for.

In my mind's eye there was a beautiful chariot. It radiated with magnificent colors of bronze and gold. This chariot was being attended by a Hugh, stocky, well dressed, Centurion that had a rather puzzled look on his face.

He was in a conversation with a voice that I or he could not see. I noticed that the chariot had no wheels and could not go anywhere. I thought it strange that the Centurion was not getting out of the chariot. I heard the Centurion say to the voice; "Like this?" (Meaning that he thought the chariot would be the means of transportation the Centurion might take).

The voice very softly spoke back to him; no, not that way." The Centurion stood to his feet, but his legs would not move forward. He called out to the voice; "Like this?" The voice calmly spoke back; "no, not that way."

I then saw a man try to walk up to the chariot to aid the Centurion, but the man's legs would not move. The centurion once again ask the voice; "Like this?" The voice spoke back; "no, not that way." So the Centurion sat there patiently, waiting on the voice to give directions on how he was to proceed forth.

My mind's eye was then turned to a specific scripture in the Bible. "Now an angel of the Lord spoke to Philip, saying, Arise and go toward the south along the road which goes down from Jerusalem to Gaza." "This is desert." "So he arose and went. And behold, a man of Ethiopia, a eunuch of great authority under Candace the queen of Ethiopians, who had charge of all her treasury, and had come to Jerusalem to worship, was returning. And sitting in his chariot, he was reading Isaiah the prophet." Then the Spirit said to Philip, "Go near and over take this chariot." "So Philip ran to him, and heard him reading the prophet Isaiah, and said, "Do you understand what you are reading?" And He said, "How can I, unless someone guides me?" And he asked Philip to come up and sit with him. The place in the scripture he read was this:

He was led as a sheep to the slaughter; and as a lamb before its shearer is silent, So He opened not His mouth. In His humiliation His justice was taken away, and who will declare His generation? For His life is taken from the earth."

So the eunuch answered Philip and said, "I ask you, of whom does the prophet say this, of himself or of some other man?" "Then Philip opened his mouth, and beginning at this scripture, preached Jesus to him. Now as they went down the road, they came to some water, And the eunuch said, "See here is water. What hinders me from being baptized?" Now when they came up out of the water, the Spirit of the Lord caught Philip away, so that the eunuch saw him no more; and he went on his way rejoicing." "But Philip was found at Azotus. And passing through, he preached in all the cities till he came to Caesarea." Once the eunuch had the wisdom of the word, he was able to move on. When Philip was obedient to do as the Lord wanted him to do, he too was able to move on in the Spirit.

Then I heard the Lord say, "You can have all the knowledge in the world but if you don't have the vehicle of wisdom to bring it forth, it will not come."

Then I was taken to another place of scripture, still seeing all this in my mind's eye. It was in Ezekiel the first chapter. Ezekiel is at the River called Chebar and Ezekiel sees visions.(Even though the vision's would just be too long to record in this writing, I so hope that it will be read by all who read this piece.) My focus was on the wheel with-in the wheel, and the fire that was being moved throughout the vision in the midst of the cherubs and the wheel. There was a voice in verse 25 that made me think of the voice I was hearing in my vision. I believe it was one in the same, in spite of the fact that I could not hear the voice in Isaiah's visions.

I could see knowledge moving up and down and sideways much like the wheel moving in the vision Isaiah had. Wisdom was the vehicle for which knowledge was able to move freely any way the Lord desired. In verse 20, it says, "Where ever the spirit wanted to go, they went, because there the spirit went; and the wheels were lifted together with them, for the spirit of the living creatures was in the wheels." Now all of a sudden, as I wrote this, I began to see that the word spirit was written with a small s. whenever you see the

Spirit of the Lord written, it is written with the big S. I think this spirit is man's spirit.

When we know what the Lord wants us to know, He always provides wisdom to move in it. If we sit at His feet and search His heart, He will give us the wisdom it takes to do what we need to do and it will take us where we need to go.

I hurried to write the vision down so that none of it would be lost. I really didn't want to take any chances. I was able at that point to share it with my prayer partners. The neat thing about all this was that I was very quiet so not to disturb the prayer that was going out as I wrote down what I had seen. I was also able to listen to what was being said to the Father. I could relate to the prayers though the vision I was having.

I feel this vision was given to us to tell us that we must not try to do anything in in our own strength. Man always likes to do things his way. What we are going to see is God move in the direction He wants to go and as He gives us the wisdom to move with the knowledge of the word of God, We will move in the direction He wants us to go. I am expecting big things to happen as we wait on the Lord. He has not allowed us to move because we were trying to do it our way, not His!

The Lady in Waiting

SHE WASN'T ATTRACTIVE, SHE DIDN'T wear a lot of make-up, she didn't have nice fine cloths, she didn't wear expensive jewelry, and she was pretty unrefined. You could say that she was a work in progress.

The cloths that she wore were badly wrinkled, and dirty. They smelled like she had been on the streets for quite some time, and there were spots all over her cloths. Her hair seemed to flow down her back, it was a beautiful copper color and with just a little help, it could glisten in the Son.

People didn't like to be around her, especially those who really knew her. There was a day when she tried to cover up what she really was. She wore nice fine cloths, she said all the right things, but her public self and her private self weren't the same. When she was in public she was one way and when she was behind closed doors she was another. Those that she felt close enough to let in, realized early on that she was not at all what she appeared to be.

This ladies ancestor's came from all over. I guess you could say she was a "Heinz 57"and if you went back in time to find her roots, they may have been very hard to track, but there was something in her that made you want to polish her and put her through the lapidary. Deep inside that hard nasty interior was something that made her worth saving.

People have no idea why she acts the way she does. I'm not sure myself and I'm one that claims to know her pretty good. Not all of her, just a small part, and yet It is still a mystery to me. She doesn't mean to do the things she does. If fact if you were to ask her, she would tell you that more than anything, she would like to change to be what she knows she someday will become.

This lady hasn't come to the realization that she smells and looks like she does. She thinks she is rich and has it altogether. She thinks she has need of nothing. Little does she know that she is poor, wretched, miserable, blind and naked, at least in the eyes of the Lord.

The sad thing about her is that she is the Bride of Christ. Her self-righteousness is as filthy rags in His sight. She has been His bride in waiting since He died on Calvary. There has been plenty of time for her to get her act together, but it seems that it has taken much longer than expected for that to happen. I know that Jesus is coming back for a bride without spot or wrinkle. Like I said before, she is a work in progress. The Lord has been working on us for centuries. There is going to come a day when the Lord shows up and we are going to be non-recognizable. The spots and wrinkles will be gone and the bride will come forth in all her glory and splendor. It puts tears in my eyes to think of how we will look to our precious bridegroom the day He lays eyes on us in our perfection. No longer will we appear to be one thing and be another. We will at that time be, honest, trustworthy, loving and dependable. We will no-longer be back biting, vicious, non- caring, having our own selfish desires.

Here's one thing that concerns me. We don't like ourselves very much. We try hard to stay away when Sunday morning comes. We sure don't like to show up when work needs to be done, or worse, when Saturday morning prayer group meets, or anytime they meet for that matter. I know it's hard for the world to want to be around us. We haven't been too people friendly, but Gods working on that. Those of our own household,(that is the Household of God) don't want to be there either. It must break Jesus' heart to think that people don't love or accept His bride.

I heard a man say once, "If you're going to come over to my house, watch a football game on my T.V. and eat my food, you had better accept that my wife is going to be there and treat her right, or me and you are going to have some trouble." Isn't that how Jesus must feel when people don't want to be around the body of Christ? In spite of the fact, she's not all that attractive, and yes, she really needs a lot of work, she is still His bride, and He loves her, and He is coming back for her once she has some things taken care of.

I can see the world not getting this, but if we claim to be a part of His body, then we have to come together in order for Him to be able to return and claim the bride He is intending to take to the New Jerusalem. In order for that to happen, we have to start liking each other, in spite of how we are now looking, acting, or smelling. Yes the self-righteous rags must come off, and yes the attitude has to change, so who needs to start the change? I don't know for sure but I think it might need to start with me.

Lately the Lord has been showing me that I have had some sarcasm that needs to be extracted. I noticed it the other day when I was talking to my boss. It wasn't as if I even really understood it for what it was, but when I began thinking about our conversation, It was very apparent that I was disrespectful to her. That wasn't my intention, but the further we got into our conversation, the worse it got. Hey, if you're reading this, I'm sorry boss, I'm learning. Then I was watching T.V. and realized that I was being sarcastic with the people on T.V. who couldn't even hear me, that didn't matter, the Lord wants it stopped. Then I was in a conversation with my prayer partners, and one of them was talking about some people they were talking to, and I made a sarcastic remark again. That is enough, the Lord has been working on me to see that sarcasm is on its way out. He can't use me that way and I can't afford to let it go on. I'm changing, and I had better, or the Lord might never return.

I hope the ones that are reading this will get it. We are not perfect! When God is finished with us, we will not be able to be recognized. Thank God for it to. If people will just be patient and longsuffering, It will all change. I know it, I just know it.

The Thief of Time

It's 2 in the morning and the T.V. has been on all day. The children are sleeping, the dog needs out the husband hasn't come home yet. Sleep has escaped the one who needs it the most because of a busy day that begins at 6 a.m.

The news flashes across the screen, the volume's been turned down, as not to wake the children. People are driving by. Where could people be going so early in the morning? The alarm rings signaling it is time to get the kids off to school.

I drag myself down the steps and realize that hubby has come in sometime in the middle of the night. What could possibly be more important than your family in the night hours. my mind thinks of something else, bringing the thoughts that really want to come to the surface captive, punishing them and sending them out of the mind.

The morning begins, I get the kids off to school. The laundry is piled up to the ceiling and I don't have the energy to get it to the washer, and if I do, then there is always drying and folding that has to be done. The house looks like a tornado has wreaked havoc on my living room and the thought of the kitchen sink, makes me want to crawl underneath the blankets that was left on the couch the night before.

The groceries have to be bought and there is no money for rent let alone food. The soap operas will be coming on soon so I need to hurry and get what I'm going to get done before they are on, or it will never get done. The nice thing about soap operas is, that you can watch them once a month and know what's going on all year long.

Before I know it the day is over and I have found myself in a cycle that I can't seem to get off of. This is insane. I expect different results, yet I do the same thing day in and day out. I wonder what people did before T.V. and video games?

Sometimes I just like to drive around and think. It helps me not to get overwhelmed by the redundant life I have lived for so many years.

This used to be me before I got saved. I never seemed to have enough hours in a day. Time was spent on everything and anything except the things that could make a difference in my life. Now I look and I see the generations coming up after me with the same problem, only worse. More videos, more things on T.V. more things to do inside and outside to keep us from getting to the really important things like prayer and reading the Word of God.

If I was to ask people how much of their day was spent on spiritual things I wonder what the answer would be. I'm not talking about secular worldly people, I'm talking about Christians who claim to know the Father.

When I first got saved I would spent literally hours in prayer and reading the Word. People told me I was a fanatic and my husband told me that if he was to bust my head open, little bibles would fall out all over the floor. I would pray awhile, then I would wait on the Lord to speak to me. I would read His Word trying so hard to find the things I needed to get me through the day. My dad was glad, because he was afraid I would become a bar fly.

Most people thought I was just a religious fanatic. I look back now and I would not give for the time I spent in His presence. I learned so much from Him in my early years that set a foundation for what I'm going through now. It is the best investment of my time that I could have ever spent. The only thing I regret is that I let people talk me out of continuing it." People have a way of laughing you into hell but they can't laugh you out." I don't remember where I heard that before, but it's the truth.

Now, I can say that I have gotten back into spending more time in the word and prayer. I love spending time with the Father. It is riches that I have stored up in Heaven," where rust and moth can't destroy." I know that's not what is meant by that scripture, but it seems to fit just the same.

I daydream sometimes of me getting to Heaven and the Lord is standing there with His ball bat and He hits me in the head and those bibles fall out all over the floor. He then smiles and says to me, "Enter in to the Joy of the Lord my precious one.

I know people don't understand what's coming. If they did, they would spent more time preparing instead of sitting day in and day out in front of the T.V. set. That's what happened in Noah's day. They were just minding their business and didn't seem to be concerned that Noah had warned them that the day was coming when there would be a flood on the earth and when it happened if they weren't prepared they would be destroyed. They didn't listen and look what happened. The flood came, the doors of the Ark closed and the people drowned. They had laughed at Noah. They didn't know what rain was. How did Noah? He spent time with the one who could make the difference and save his life. And the life of others had they not judged him a nut case. (I'll talk more of Noah latter, in another story.)

They might argue in the end, that they didn't have the Word of God as we do these days, so will we be more accountable? The Word tells us that just like in the days of Noah, destruction is coming. Not by flood but by fire. Who will listen?

The Bible is an amazing piece. It is as though every time I read it I see something new. It's been thirty years since I've got saved. I have never grown tired of reading the Word or finding new things in it every time I read it.

Someday the Lord will return and I will be ready. I laugh at times when I tell people that I have rapture practice. My time is spent more wisely now than it used to be. I don't want to have to stand before the Lord and have to give an account for the time I had wasted.

Ears to Hear

My grandson was born on August 12th 2008. I had the honor of watching him when his mother went back to work. He was especially pleasant, and I was extremely grateful that he was. I would rock him, and sing to him and he loved to cuddle.

When he was old enough to latch on to my ear, he would take a handful and just stare at me as though he was listening intently. I would sit in the rocker waiting for him to finish listening and I would think it very strange that he did that.

Gavin just turned two and he still comes running to me, motioning for me to pick him up and when I do, he grabs both ears and turns his head slightly to one side or the other. He doesn't want to talk, he won't answer me if I talk to him, he just wants to listen.

Many times I am like that with the Father. I will go to Him, and I do not want to say anything, I just want to listen. It takes a while for me to hear things some times, so I don't hurry away if I don't hear something right away. I know if I wait, I will not go away disappointed.

In the book of Revelation Jesus sends a message to 7 churches. At the end of every message He says the same thing, "He who has an ear, let him hear." I think this is pretty important. There's more to it then listening with a human ear. Jesus wants the churches to have a revelation of what He is saying. Often things have more than one meaning, especially when it comes to the Word of God.

There is a saying I remember hearing a lot, it went like this, "Read between the lines." There are hidden meanings that are buried with-in scripture that you have to dig for. That's why Jesus spoke to people in parables. Mark 4:11 says, " To you it has been given to know the mystery of the kingdom of God; but to those who are outside, all things come in parables, so that seeing they may see and not perceive, and hearing they may hear and not understand; Lest they should turn, and their sins be forgiven them." He didn't always want everyone to know what He was talking about. Sometimes the things He said were for the chosen few that he connected with, or those that would take the time to listen to what He had to say.

God has a lot to say in His Word about hearing and listening, someone once said, " God gave us two ears and only one mouth, because He wanted us to do twice as much listening and only half as much talking." In Matt. 13:13 he even talks about those who hear, but don't hear. In Heb. 5:11 He talks about those who grow dull of hearing.

Jesus has a way of keeping those who don't know Him from hearing His voice., He says of them, "Everyone who is of the truth hears my voice." If you don't walk in truth, you will not hear His voice.

Jesus often commanded His people to hear Him. Deut. 6:4, "Hear, O Israel!" "Hear, you who are afar!" Is. 33:13, "Hear O heavens." Is. 1:2. It's so important that we listen.

The Lord also wants you to be careful what you hear. Mark 4:24 says, " Take heed what you hear. With the same measure you use, it will be measured to you; and to you who hear, more will be given. Verse 25, "For whoever has, to him more will be given; but whoever does not have, even what he has will be taken from him." We have a responsibility to train ourselves to hear the voice of God, Hearing isn't just there for whatever comes our way, It is vital that we pay special attention to what we hear and who we hear it from. This type of hearing is known as, "spiritual perception." "Those who receive and assimilate truth will have their capacity enlarged and their knowledge increased." We can't afford to continue in ignorance.

Matt. 18:15 talks about those who don't want to hear. Sometimes we know what we are to do but when someone wants to tell us when we are in error, we don't want to hear what they have to say, even though they know that it is the truth. They have mindsets that cause them to think one way in-spite of the fact that they know the truth, but don't want to walk in it. It's hard when I know that I'm being corrected at those times.

I feel like Gavin will be a good listener when He grows up. I also feel that God has a special call on his life. If I know him like I think I do, he will grab a hold of the ears of God and not let go until the Father listens.

Sweet Spirit

WHEN YOU'RE JUST A LITTLE girl and someone at school gives you a hard time, it makes you feel like your world is coming to an end. That's how my daughter used to feel when she would get picked on at school.

The day would end and I would tuck my sweet baby girl into bed and together we would say our prayers. It would make me so sad to hear the cries of a broken hearted child plead with the Father to make the day go by fast if it was going to be a bad one. But if the day was going to go good, then she would pray that the Father let it last a long time. Never once did I ever hear her ask for her not to have to go through the things that she had to go through as kids would be mean to her.

I wanted to go to school and tramp on their face, but she would be so longsuffering and be kind. The worse they treated her, the nicer she was to them. I just didn't know where that was coming from. It had to be coming from the Holy Spirit, because I wasn't teaching her to be kind to them. I have just started getting the concept of it all in the last 6 months. Not her, she has always been able to look past someone's shortcomings and love them anyway.

Before it was over, the kids that would be picking on her would end up being her best friends. It would really blow my mind to see God work it out that way for her. He was honoring her for the way she treated people.

We are not accountable for the way people treat us, but we are however responsible for the way we treat others, and she got that very early on. She is still like that today. I don't mean that she is a door matt and that she lets people run over her. She actually knows how to put someone in their place if she has to, but for the most part she is very respectful and kind.

Amber is a very strong woman. She is a great mother and a wonderful daughter. She is my, "Proverbs 31 woman." I would speak that over her daily as she would run in and out of the house, bringing in the underdogs of the town, so she could love them and care for them.

I wonder how she will fare when her little one goes off to school and comes home for the first time having his feelings hurt because he is a very tender sweet soft spoken child too. I have a feeling that she will continue to allow the Holy Spirit to speak through her as she tells him to be patient and they will someday come around to be his friend.

The world is full of bullies. Today it seems worse than it used to be. Kids are actually killing themselves because of the bullying they are experiencing. I still have little patience when I hear of someone picking on another, big or small it doesn't matter. The Lord is doing a work in me but I'm far from there yet.

God very seldom lets us go around a situation when it's hard. He will always go through it with us, but never the less we still have to go through it.

"But now, thus says the Lord, who created you, O Jacob, fear not, And He who formed you O Israel, Fear not, for I have redeemed you, I have called you by your name, you are mine. When you pass through the waters, I will be with you; and through the rivers, they shall not overflow you, when you walk through the fire, you shall not be burned. Nor shall the flame scorch you. For I am the Lord your God, The Holy One of Israel your Savior; I gave Egypt for your ransom, Ethiopia and Seba in your place .Since you were precious in my sight, you have been honored." Isaiah 43:1-5.

There is a story in the Old Testament about a wicked king who bullied someone for some property he had. The king wanted his neighbor's field because it was next door to his land and he wanted it for a vegetable garden. That land was that man's inheritance and he wasn't willing to part from it. The land was very precious to him. The king who had everything that he could ever possibly want, pouted because Naboth would not sell the land to him.

The king's wife took matters into her own hands and forged letters in the king's name to the men of the city, accusing Naboth of blaspheming God and had Naboth stoned so that the king could have the land that belonged to Naboth.

The Lord didn't allow the king to get away with what he did and it cost him his life. God has a way of dealing with bullies. If he did it for Naboth, He will do it for anyone else who gets bullied. I'm glad my children are grown. It's painful to see them suffer when someone chooses to bully them, but it's nice to know that the Father is on our side, not allowing bullies to have the last word!

My Favorite Quarterback

I HATE PAIN! IT HAS never been one of my favorite things to have to go through. In fact I am a pansy when it comes to pain. The Lord tells me that I can't be a coward. When I go through pain because of something, I'm very careful from that point on, not to let the same things happen to me if I can help it.

My oldest son was playing football one year, and broke both bones in his leg. He had to have a cast that went all the way up his leg. The Doctor was afraid that it would do a lot of damage to the growth plate and that it would affect his performance as a football player.

I wanted so bad for my son to say that he was never going to play football again, but that didn't happened. He was so brave, as soon as he could get back out on the field, he was there. It made me very nervous and I wasn't happy about it, but I knew it was the right thing for him to do and he did it. He didn't allow a painful setback keep him from doing what he loved to do.

The Apostle Paul said, "I press toward the goal for the prize of the upward call of God in Christ Jesus." (Phil. 3:14). Paul was so messed up physically for believing and preaching the word. He talked about in 2 Cor.4:8-9. He said," we are hard-pressed on every side, yet not crushed, we are perplexed, but not in despair; persecuted, but not forsaken,; struck down, but not destroyed." He didn't allow anything keep him from running the race. He knew what it took to run the race but he never looked back.

Jesus said in Luke 9, "No one, having put his hand to the plow, and looking back, is fit for the kingdom of God." We can't afford to be cowards if we are going to live for the Lord. We do however, need to know what we are getting ourselves into before we begin.

Jesus says, " For which of you, intending to build a tower, does not sit down first and count the cost, whether he has enough to finish it, lest after he has laid the foundation, and is not able to finish, all who see it begin to mock him, saying, this man began to build and was not able to finish." (Luke 14:28-29.

My son knew when he started to play football that there would be times when he would get hurt. He was willing to take that chance because it was sometime he thought was worth the pain. And I knew when I became a Christian that there would be persecution from the world, but I think it's worth what I have to go through to preach Jesus and Him crucified.

Alignment

I WASN'T SURE I COULD make friends again with anyone. I thought I could never trust again. I had been in some pretty bad relationships with those I thought I could put my life in their hands, but I learned later to be very careful who I align myself with.

Early in my walk as a Christian, I wanted so badly to fit in and to make friends. It felt important to be with the people in the church that was important. I wanted to surround myself with people I thought were healthy and on fire for the Lord.

People are too often not what you think they are. When you really get to know them behind closed doors, they tend to show their true colors. I was stunned with the truth in more than one situation. I wanted to give the benefit of the doubt, but I found myself thinking, "What have I got myself into?"

I won't go into who it was that shocked me into reality. But it helps me to understand why the Bible says, "I marvel that you are turning away so soon from Him who called you in the grace of Christ, to a different gospel which is not another, but there are some who trouble you and want to pervert the gospel of Christ. But even if we, or an angel from heaven, preach any other gospel to you than what we have preached to you, let him be accursed. As we have said before, so now I say again, if anyone preaches any other gospel to you than what you have received, let him be accursed. For do I now persuade men, of God? Or do I seek to please men, would not be a bondservant of Christ." (Gal. 1:6-10).

I have learned that it doesn't matter if you have been friends all your life with someone, they can still become deceived by the world without knowing that they have been deceived. If that's the case it's not a matter of you trying to lead them to the truth, it becomes a matter that the Holy Spirit will have to deal with them about.

I was so deceived, that it took me fasting 56 days (It was the Daniel's fast) for the Lord to show me the truth about what I had gotten myself into. This mess was so sensitive, that I can't even say what it was that I had endured at the hands of those who I had considered close friends and brothers and sisters in the Lord.

I will say that it caused me to lose everything I had, including my husband. But although I lost everything, it did wake me up to the fact that I must be very careful to know who I am to align myself with.

There is a way to be sure that you are in right relationships. I'm sorry that I learned this very late in my Christian walk. There is a kindred spirit that witnesses in your spirit when you come in contact with those that you know you can trust. There is also a red flag inside when you are in the presence of someone who confesses to be serving God but is not. I am guilty of knowing of this flag and yet not allowing it to speak. I pushed it down inside thinking it was just me and my way of thinking. I will not be so easily deceived next time. I will from now on listen to my gut feeling. I paid a big price to learn that lesson.

Thank God that the word helps us to know what to do. In Proverbs it talks about getting Godly council and how there is safety in doing that. (Proverbs 24:6) When I went to my pastor and told him what was going on, it was clear that he was in agreement with what I should do. He was wise in sharing his heart and I am thankful that he wasn't "too close to the forest to see the trees," so to speak.

I love the body of Christ. We need each other, but there are those in the body who are sick. They are so sick with deception; they don't realize they are sick because somehow the enemy has been able to blind them to the truth. I pray for them and I speak blessings on them that somehow they will have their eyes opened to the truth and will be set free before it is too late.

The Power of Praise

I CAN'T BELIEVE THAT I have served the Lord for 30 years and I'm just getting the revelation of praise and what it is capable of doing. I've read all the scriptures, I sing daily to the Lord, I sing sometimes at church, and I love it when those who have a talent, pour their heart out before the Lord in song. Lately I have been listening closer to the songs that are played on Christian radio, to see if the songs are songs of praise, or if they are songs that demand and expect things from the Lord. I'm very happy that I hear a lot of praise going on and worship too.

I've been attending a bible study on prayer and I was surprised when the writer of the material talked about praise and worship, being a form of prayer. I always thought it was a whole different thing. I also attend an intercessory prayer group on Saturday mornings, and I think about the role I play there. It seems that when I start praying, I go immediately to praise. I have often told myself that instead of calling it intercessory prayer, I need to call it intercessory praise.

There are stories about people who have been praying for others and nothing seems to work, then when praise comes from someone's mouth, things start happening. I then realized as I was learning this, that the word says, God inhabits the praises of His people. Its one thing to read that, and quote it, but when you get a revelation it blows your mind.

Saul and Silas was imprisoned after being beaten and shackled, as they began to praise, something awesome happened, they were able to lead the jailer and others to the Lord. They were in the midst of one of the hardest times of their lives and they chose to praise the Lord.

God inhabited their praise as they sang in the midst of their suffering. Never under estimate the power of praise, especially in the times that seem to be the darkest. What happened during that great event was earth shattering, literally, there was an earthquake that got the attention of not only the prisoners that were there with them, but also the jailer who almost took his own life because the prison door were opened and they just knew that Saul and Silas had escaped.

It wasn't until Saul shouted out that they were all present and accounted for, that the jailer put his sword down. It was very dark where they were, and as the jailer called for light to see, he experienced a light that would never allow him ever to have to walk in darkness again, for he was going to meet the light of the world and his whole life was going to change. Not only was he saved but his whole household.

Immediately, he changed the way he treated his prisoner's. He took them and cleaned them up and treated their wounds and gave them something decent to eat. The Lord had not only saved them, but baptized them and dressed them for service. (Acts 16:25-34).

The concordance in my bible says, "Since God is enthroned in the praises, worship is the key to entering fully into His presence. That concept here is that praise releases Gods glory, thus bringing to the worshipers actualized responses of His kingly reign. His enthroned responses through the Holy Spirit can take many forms, such as prophecy, healings, miracles, affirmation to individual hearts, a call to reverential silence and awe, conviction of sin, and salvation of sinners." (Psalms 22:3 commentary). No wonder the jailer and his household were saved and the prison doors were opened.

I will never offer praise the same way ever again. I know now, that there is more than just power in praise, I now praise with the knowledge that God Himself is on the scene, and when God shows up things happen!

I don't want to just praise God because of the things that happen when we praise Him. I truly think He is deserving of our praise. He doesn't receive as much of it as He is due. I heard a song yesterday that said, "I would like to sing a praise to you that you are worthy of but, I can't because it would have to be endless" and that is so true, but wouldn't it please Him if someone would just try!

I know that we will never be able to give God what He deserves, at least not while we are here on earth, but it makes me understand how that the angels cried Holy, Holy, Holy, throughout eternity in the Book of Revelation. He is worthy for them to do so. Someone once said that, "the reason they did that is because every time they circled the throne, they were able to see a new aspect of who God was." That's awesome!

I may never be able to give God all the praises that He is due, but I'm glad that I will have eternity to try.

Ministering for the Lord

I SAT AT MY DINING room table and thought about how little I had done for the Lord. How could I, being what I was, really do anything that would minister for Him? "The people I go to church with don't really know me, and if they did, they wouldn't like who I really am," That's what I have always told myself. I had been the kind of person that was really rough around the edges.

Left to myself, I am wretched. The only thing that makes me anything, is who Jesus is in me. So imagine how surprised I was when someone had asked me to speak at their ladies meeting. I was very young in the Lord and I had no idea that the Lord looked at all of us in the same light. I really didn't know that when the Father looked at us, all He sees is the blood of His awesome precious Son.

I felt overwhelmed and wished I could go back and ask them if they could get someone else to speak. At the same time, I did have something to say. I was used up pretty bad, I was a bit of a red neck, and I was like that man that stood beside the Pharisee and beat his chest , not even able to look up as he prayed. (Luke 18:10-14) He cried out, "God be merciful to me a sinner!" I could identify with this guy. We both knew what we were. It's shameful, the things we do. How God was ever able to sift through all that sin and be able to see us as worth dying for is amazing to me, but He did!

The only way that I could relate what I was feeling to these ladies, was to share with them a poem that the Lord had put on my heart. It wasn't anything that I thought would move people, but it was my heart and it was how I thought the Father saw me. I guess it was my way to fit in, or maybe it was Gods way of showing me that I had my own special place in His heart.

As I sit here and write this, I can't help but to think of the beautiful scripture in Malachi 3 where it says that we will be His jewels. God is the only one who can talk something so common and ugly and broken, and turn it into a precious jewel.

It came time for me to speak to the ladies of the church. I have a dear friend who has been a rock in my life since we met over twenty years ago. She invited me to this church and for a minute, I was able to worship with her there. It was during that time that I presented my little poem. It goes something like this:

"Crystal sets upon a shelf, a beauty to behold. It sparkles like a diamond, whether new or old. And sometimes it's forgotten and rarely ever used, it's just a dust collector and never really used. The coffee cup is different, it's used most every day, it's stained, and cracked, or broken and common most would say. It isn't made for beauty, or to sit upon a shelf. In constant need of cleansing, it's made just like myself. And so I ask the Savior, which one was made for me, He said "the coffee cup is the one you ought to be."

I was so nervous about speaking that I could hardly read the poem. I tried to get the point across that we don't have to be perfect for God to want to use us. He wants us to come as we are, then He will perfect us in His time.

The night seemed to be a big hit. I got a lot of comments on my teaching and it encouraged me to continue to share as the Father gave me things I thought needed said. Today I speak a lot. I travel and speak, enjoying every minute of the time I get to share. I'm still a coffee cup. God has glued me, cleaned me over and over and over again and keeps filling me up with His word. I love it when others can enjoy drinking from my cup. I wouldn't change places with anyone for anything in the world. I love my journey with the Lord.

The Lord has always encouraged me to use visuals. I was in a meeting one night, again speaking some of what I felt the Lord was giving me to share. I was sharing about discernment and how important it is in the body of Christ to be able to be those watchmen on the wall. I wanted to get the point across, that if we see something that others may not be aware of, that we should shout it from the roof top so that the enemy of our souls will not be successful at destroying us.

I really wanted to get this point across in a way that the women would not forget what I was sharing. We were meeting at my Sunday school teacher's house and his wife was a picture of a lamb, so gentle and so sweet. I wasn't sure how she was going to accept this, so I did the wise thing and told her in advance, what it was that I was going to be sharing. She was a real trooper, and let me proceed.

It was time to begin, and everyone was to get a bite to eat while they were waiting. There was quite a spread of food and I was in charge of making the pudding. It was chocolate. One of the ladies came in and scooped up a big spoonful of the pudding and gathered a few other items and put them on her plate. She put her spoon into the pudding and took a big bite. She slowly sat her plate down, swallowed hard, and set there quietly, trying to figure out what had happened to the pudding.

Another lady came in and filled her plate with just about everything that sat on the table, went into the living room and reclined in her chair, almost as if she was nesting. You could see that she was getting ready to have a feast. She opened her mouth and put a large spoonful of the pudding into her mouth and as fast as it went in, it returned to the plate, as she screamed, "don't anyone eat the pudding!" I chuckled and looked at our host with great delight. I had gotten my point across without having to say a word. (I told you I was wretched, left to myself).

The topic for the evening was discernment and if you were to choose one part of your body that helps you to discern it would be the nose. Had anyone thought to smell the pudding, it would have been a dead giveaway. My recipe was dark cocoa with miracle whip. It must have tasted horrible. It looked like pudding. It had the same consistency and the color was just beautiful, but the taste was enough to have this lady warn the next door neighbors with one big scream.

I shared how we are supposed to let others know when there is a problem, even when we think that we might hurt someone's feelings doing it. Too many times the enemy has been able to deceive us because he works through those he doesn't think we will question. We don't want to offend others, but if what is happening will bring harm to the body of Christ, then our priority is to tell what we know. In doing so, we might even help the one bringing the danger.

Now, the first lady who ate the pudding did nothing to warn others not to eat it, because she didn't want to hurt my feelings. The other didn't care, it tasted bad enough to her that she didn't want others to have to experience it.

I would rather have someone hurt my feelings, and do the right thing, rather than stand by and just watch what is going down. The woman who was the watchman on the wall had a good sense of humor, so she didn't hold the incident against me, although she did say that she wouldn't trust my cooking any longer. I think I got my point across, because no one else ate the pudding, and that girl made lots of friends that night.

Since that visual worked so well, I thought I would try it again at a youth gathering at the Methodist church, where I was serving as a youth director. We were going to have a contest and the pastor insisted on joining us. It was a perfect opportunity for the kids to get a good laugh and for me at the same time to teach a lesson.

It would be a contest of the pastor against the children. He loved pudding and he was a big eater, he also was quite competitive. I prepared the pudding and sat it down in front of the children before giving my special recipe to the pastor. When I said go, the children, at the same time as the pastor dug in and were eating away. The pastor had the strangest look on his face as he watched the children wolf down the pudding without difficulty. The pastor however could not finish the race. He couldn't understand how those children could enjoy that horrible taste the way they did. He was not a happy camper when he realized that he had been deceived. He did however forgive me when he realized that it went with the teaching on discernment. He would never eat my cooking again, but he would listen to the things I spoke on. It also has taught him to be very careful what he puts in his mouth from now on.

The Lord has truly blessed me with the ability to take nothing and make something out of it. If given the chance, I can relate anything that is given to me with some sort of lesson. I love visuals and I have used them for as long as I can remember.

Regardless of whether we are called to be watchman on the wall or to just share a poem, it's good to know that everyone is capable of ministering for the lord.

Flipping Houses

DALLAS, TEXAS IS ONE OF the most beautiful places that one can ever imagine. I remember traveling there for the first time by airplane. I was visiting my dad who lived in Fairfield, Texas. I thought the skyline was the most breath taking thing that I had ever seen.

I was picked up at the airport and transported late at night, so the city was lit up like Christmas. I could not have imagined it any more beautiful than it was. I really didn't get to appreciate it for what it was because my dad lived quite a distance from Dallas, and we had a long way to go to get there, so I didn't get to hang out there very long.

The year was 1981 and I was 20 years old. I had hardly ever been out of the state of Ohio and I was quite impressed with the size of the city. For the next 25 years, I would find myself moving back and forth from Ohio to Texas, and you might say I had a love affair with the south. I loved the people there and was infatuated with the state for many reasons. All those years of traveling back and forth I really didn't have a clear understanding about the city of Dallas as a whole.

It wasn't until my last move there several years ago, that I would get a different perspective of the city as I now know it. For two years my husband and I worked there flipping houses.

We lived in Corsicana Texas, which is 50 miles south of Dallas. Every day we would wake up and pack a lunch and drive to Dallas and the surrounding towns to work on houses that needed restored.

These houses were the most disgusting places I have ever seen. We would, most of the time, go in and tear out each house all the way back to the studs. Once the house was stripped of everything but the studs, we would begin to put the house back together. This meant that we would have to go to the nearest home improvement store and load the truck with all the things we needed to finish what job we would be working on that week. I got so sick of walking into those types of stores that sometimes I would just refuse to go in, and so I would stay in the truck dreading what kind of day we were going to have.

The work was hard and most of the time I had no idea what I was doing. I would use my imagination and do the work the best way I knew how and it always seemed to work out, but it was often frustrating and always filthy. In fact it was the filthiest work that I have ever done in my whole life.

There were times when I wondered what offal thing that I had done that I would have to be punished enough to have to do the work that I was doing. Every day I would think to myself, " What have I gotten myself into." I made a promise that if I ever got myself out of that job, I would never work in that line of work again.

There were times when I thought, how could a husband let his wife step foot in a place like this, let alone work 14 hour days, sweating and hurting every hour of the day as I did.

Most of the time, we were the only ones working on the house. Occasionally, there would be people come in and level the house, or work on the electric, but for the most part it was just him and I. We would often work until it was too dark to see. Most of the time there was no electricity or running water or we would have probably worked longer.

I would come into our house at the end of the day after traveling an hour to get home and I would have cramps so bad in my legs that I couldn't sleep at night. My husband and I would sit in the truck for a while, because we didn't have the strength to get out and go into the house.

These houses we had to work on were almost to the point that the city should have condemned them. At one point the boss came in to view one of the houses that we were to work on and he had to go outside because he thought he was going to throw up. The smell was so bad that we needed to wear masks to work in the house. The rat droppings were so bad in the house that we had to shovel them into large size trash bags before we started to remodel the place.

As we began to tear away at the damaged dry wall in the ceiling, I had to dodge the rats that fell from the ceiling as my husband demolished what was left of the ceiling. This house actually took longer than we had expected because it was so damaged. It wouldn't have been so bad if the houses we worked on would have been cleaned out by the previous owners before we began, but that was almost never the case.

One time the men who were hired to level a house we were working on, were under the house and rolled in human dung because some squatters had took up residence in the house and didn't have water to flush the toilet, so

110

they squatted down on the floor and took care of their business in a hole that had been in the bathroom floor.

Another time we were sent out to work on a house that had been a Meth lab. There were hypodermic needles everywhere, even in the attic. One of the electricians got stuck with one of them and was so afraid that he was going to get aids, that he quit and we never heard from him again. We went through 3 electricians at that house, not because of the needles but because of the snakes that were in the attic. We finally hired someone to come in and exterminate the snakes before we could finish remodeling the house.

The yard at that residence, had an underground pool that had to be fixed. Once we cleaned out the back yard that was waist high with trash, It actually was a very nice place for someone to live. Between the snakes, the spiders, and the hypodermic needles, I thought I was going to have a nervous breakdown.

Flees were always a problem too. One house we restored had flees so bad that we would have to bomb it each day before we could actually go in and get any work done, and that was after we had the exterminator there. They were under the house and we couldn't get rid of them. I finally ask my boss if I could borrow his dog. When he ask why, I told him I wanted to use the dog, so flees would bite the dog instead of me. He said he wouldn't do that to his dog. That made me sad that he would expect me to go into places that he wouldn't allow his dog to go.

Painting outside in the middle of summer was a real challenge for me. It was 110 degrees one day and my paint was so thick, it was like butter. The sun was so hot that I was dehydrated to the point that I had horrible cramps in my legs and my feet swelled to the point that you couldn't see my ankles.

Every day was a new adventure. I never knew what I was going to see or have to do on any given day. I laid tile, dry walled, painted, helped with the plumbing, the list went on and on. I truly believe that if I had to, I could build a house without a whole lot of help.

The happiest day of those two years, (except for the day I found out that I was coming home) was the day that the boss laid me off and made my husband do the work himself and hire outside help when he needed it. No one should ever be exposed to some of the things we were exposed to.

I remember the day we had rented a wet saw to cut tile I was installing in a kitchen. We were in the worst part of Dallas, where there had been people killed just down the street. We really had to watch our backs at this place. My step son was visiting us and offered to help out. We were getting ready to stop for the day and we were cleaning up when he ask his dad where the saw went. Here, someone came and stole the saw right out from under our noses. The very next week they came back and stole six hundred dollars' worth of tools from the bedroom while my husband worked in another room. That was the last job that I had worked on. It was all I could take to make it that far. It was really getting dangerous.

Speaking of dangerous, one of the first houses we remodeled, exploded right after we completed work on it. It looked like someone had set off a bomb. The gas line had something wrong with it and when the gas was turned on it blew-up. The insurance company thought it might be an insurance job, but that was not the case.

After having to work in the places we worked, I have never looked at Dallas the same since. There is a side to that place that people with money have never seen. I guess it's like that in every big city in the world.

God was with me every day that I showed up on that job. I can be thankful that He doesn't allow us to go through more than we can bear, but there were times when I wondered just how much I could stand. I know there was a reason for it, but for now, I'm not sure what it is.

I'm getting ready to build a big house. I think all that I learned in the south will come in handy for that very reason. At least the place I will be working on will be new. I won't have to worry about bats and rats and things like that!

Fear

I WAS AWAKENED TO FIND that I was trembling with fear. I was paralyzed to the point where I couldn't even turn on the light to see where the strange noise was coming from. The vibration was near my head and even after knowing that it was coming from outside, it was still too close for comfort. I finally got up the courage to find the switch on the lamp near my bed. I turned on the light and felt like I had accomplished a great task. To be free from that fear was very liberating.

I then got out of bed and looked out my window, afraid of what I might see, but curious enough that I had to look out. Much to my surprise was a cow butted up against my trailer kicking it with his foot. It was the strangest thing I ever experienced. I didn't know if I should feel mad or relieved. Relief won out and the cow lived.

Since it was the middle of the night and I had small children that would be rising up early in the morning, I really wanted to go back to sleep. My bible sat on the night stand and it brought me great comfort to read what it had to say to me, to let me know it was not going to be a sleepless night. I opened it up to the passage that stated, "When you lie down you will not be afraid; yes, you will lie down and your sleep will be sweet." Proverbs 3:24. I couldn't have found it that quick again if my life would have depended on it.

The Lord knows just what you need at the very time when you need it. I'm so glad that the God I serve nether sleeps or slumbers. He is with us in the night hours as well as in the middle of the day.

There are too many times in my life that I have been very afraid. I travel 30 to 40 minutes a night home from work. One cold winter night, I started home about 12:30 and had no idea that it was cold enough to freeze the wetness on the road. I got half way home and realized that I was driving on black ice. I became very paranoid, but was too far home to turn around. I tried to inch my way home and I have to say I had the ride of my life. I ended up hitting a guardrail, a ditch, and spent half the night parked alongside the road trying to decide whether it was safe for me to continue my journey. I set most of the night, wishing daylight would come to where I could at least see where I was going and thanking God that I had not been hurt. I finally arrived home about 6 am the next morning.

I was never so glad to get home in all my life. It could have been bad. I could have flipped over that guard rail and totaled my car. I could have hit another car and killed myself or someone else, but again the Lord was with me and when it was all said and done, I had arrived home un hurt and with my car still intact, fear was there but it did not win out.

One night I was driving home and I felt very depressed. I had been very disobedient to the Lord and I was at the end of myself, literally. I was contemplating killing myself and I had thought about just waiting until a car coming head on would pass and I would change lanes putting myself and the other car in danger. The minute I thought it, a car came, if I would have just done it instead of thinking about it, I would have been badly injured or dead and so would the people in the oncoming car.

When I realized what could have happened, I became weak with fear. I had just saw my life pass before my eyes and what would have been the outcome? I had no real reason to want to take my life, but my mind was listening to the voice of the enemy that wants to destroy me. I look back on that night and see the devastation that I could have caused my husband and children. Again, I believe the Lord was there to keep it from happening.

Another time when I was just nine years old, I tried to teach myself how to swim. I dog padded out to a diving board where there were a lot on people diving. I waited and then took my turn jumping off the diving area. Before I had a chance to come up out of the water, a man dived in and landed on top of me. I thought for sure that I was going to drown. Fear came on me in such a way that I had to supernaturally find the strength to make it to the top of the water. That was probably the closest I've ever came to death. I have never cared for the water since then. God was with me that day too.

Fear comes in many ways for many reasons. Sometimes it's good to have a healthy fear of things. For instance; " The fear of the Lord is the beginning of knowledge." Proverbs 1:7. As long as your fear is not a lack of faith, then I think fear is ok, but things should not be feared when God is with you and able to keep you in all your ways. "Sometimes the only thing we had to fear is fear itself!"(President Roosevelt).

My True Addiction

From the time I was very young, I have had an addicted personality. I would drink from any bottle I could get my hands on without my parents knowing what I was doing. I was very sneaky. I could swipe a bottle of beer out from under my dad's seat while he was playing his guitar and he would never know it was missing. I would take cigarettes from my mother's cigarette pack and light them at the kitchen stove while she slept in the next room and she would never smell the smoke.

When I became a teenager I gravitated towards the gang who had the most drugs and alcohol. I would go to school and at noon get high and sleep though the rest of the afternoon classes without anyone saying anything to me.

By the time I was sixteen, I was selling marijuana to pay my electric bill. I got pregnant at sixteen and had to get married. It never dawned on me that I was an addict. I just wanted to get high. When I was twenty I got saved after my turbulent teen years. I remember thinking; why now, I'm just now turning an age when I can drink legally.

My addiction didn't stop when I got saved. I put every bit as much effort into my walk with the Lord as I ever did my drugs. I still get high from the experience I have with the Lord. I know that there's not a day goes by that I think I can make it without the Lord in my life.

Every day I wake up and know, if today is going to be worth anything, then it has to be driven by the things of the Spirit. I like it that way and I will never change it. If I have to be addicted to something then it's going to be the God of this universe that I'm addicted to.

The difference between being addicted to drugs and alcohol and being addicted to Spiritual things is that these things won't hurt you. Ok, I understand that if I end up like Jim Jones or David Karesh, then there might be problems, but it's not like that with me. I have no agenda like those guys did. I'm not on some power struggle to make a name for myself. I love the Lord with all that is with-in me.

I'm not even sure that addicted is the right word. I like to say, sold out. I think that explains it better. All I know is that I have never felt better since I've gave my life over to the one I know can take the reins and make my life better. I've tried to run my life, and I screwed it up so bad that I could have never fixed it. Life for me now has never been better. Jesus dug me up from the trenches of my addiction and found something in me that was worth saving. He calls me His Jewel and I love that!

A Walk of Faith

"Now FAITH IS THE SUBSTANCE of things hoped for, the evidence of things not seen". Hebrews 11:1 In other words, faith is something believed before you see it. It means that I am believing God for what I am hoping for, and knowing that it is already there.

I get a lot of questions when I try to walk in the things I believe God for. It's ok to question me, but please, I don't want people doubting God in the process. I can't imagine what would have happened if Noah would have doubted God when He told him to build the ark. He hadn't seen the rain yet. He didn't know that there was such a thing as rain, and the people gave Noah all kinds of heart ache about it.

I want so much to please the Father and when I know He was told me to do something and I can line it up with the word of God, I'm not going to be satisfied until I do what I know I'm supposed to do. Then I think, "what if God told me to do something and it is as of important as what He told Noah to do and I don't do it? It could mean that people's lives are at stake. I can't let the fact that others may not believe that I am hearing from God stop me.

I bet that Noah had people saying to him, "what if God isn't telling you to build that ark?" I think Noah said to them, "If God didn't tell me to build the ark, then what is it going to hurt if I do it anyway? I think He did, so I better do it. I would rather do what I think God is telling me to do and be wrong, then to not do it because there is a chance that I'm not hearing right, and miss God altogether.

In Genesis 12:1 "God tells Abram to get out of your country, from your family and from your father's house, to a land that I will show you." I bet his family was wondering if Abram really heard from God. If Abram had disobeyed God, all those blessings that He promised him would have been gone and Abram would have been in a mess. Not only would Abram missed the blessings, so would we. Gal. 3:13-14. I will not apologize for the fact that God has chosen to bless me, Financially, emotionally, physically, mentally, spiritually and every other way I can think of. All that is required of me is that I'm obedient to Him. That means I may have to do some unconventional things that others don't understand.

Right now it looks like I can't get much lower in the natural than I am. I don't have a place to live of my own, I am about to quit my job, I have no savings, I'm living pay check to pay check and I don't know from day to day where I'm going to lay my head. One thing I do know is that God said if I will be obedient to Him, that the blessings will chase me down and overtake me. (Deut. 28:2) I'm being obedient the best way I know how, and I give testimony this day that by this time next year, "I will be the head and not the tail, I will be the lender and not the borrower" (Deut. 28:13) If I continue to be obedient to the Father, and I plan to.

I know that these were promises to Abram, but I also read in Gal. 3:13-14 that these promises are also extended to me because of what Christ did at the cross. Gal. 3:29 says, "And if you are Christ's, then you are Abrahams seed, and heirs according to the promise." I love that!

Some might say, If that's true way are you in the predicament that you are in?" As an heir there are certain times appointed when the inheritance is given. (Gal. 4:2). That doesn't mean that it's not mine, it just means that the Father hasn't appointed it into my hands yet. He alone knows when I will be ready. I know this passage is speaking of Christ, but if it's talking about Christ then all the more will my inheritance be.

I know it's there and I have gladly received it even before it is in my hands, now that's faith and without faith it is impossible to please God (Hebrews 11:6). God has called me to go into all the world and preach the gospel to every creature (Luke 16:16).

I'm looking! The word means to " to look away from everything else in order to look intently on one object." Strong's #872. My eyes are on Jesus, "The author and finisher of my faith." (Hebrews 12:2).

I can rest knowing that God is with me. I have the confidence to know that if what I'm doing isn't of Him, He will let me know. He knows my heart, He knows my agenda, and that is to bring glory to His name and to bring others into the kingdom so they can do the same.

The Battle Ship

I HAD BEEN PRAISING THE Lord after coming off of midnight shift and was standing in my daughter's living room, very quiet before the Lord. I then began to see a large body of water that I believe to be an ocean. The water was very murky and cloudy. I could see part of what I believe to be a submarine sinking in slow motion. I couldn't see all of it but for some reason I knew that was what it was. It was old and small but I knew that it was deadly. I saw what appeared to be bubbles coming from it as it sank.

My attention was then directed to a large battle ship that was very still on top of the same body of water. It seemed to be anchored to the bottle of the ocean, if that's what it was. I felt as though this submarine had a bomb and that the mission of this sub, was to destroy the battle ship, but was unable for some unknown reason not to be able to complete its mission. The Battle ship didn't appear to be in distress, it was as if it knew that no harm was going to come to it.

I had a strong urge at this time to call my prayer partner and share with her what the Lord had showed me in the vision. As we talked about it, we seemed to get off the subject and on to some prayer needs that we eventually prayed for while on the phone. As we prayed the Lord had showed me that the vision wasn't just for me but was for the benefit of encouragement and I could see at that point all the different ways the enemy had covertly come against some of the people in are church. These attacks were deadly and if the enemy would have his way, those people would die. The Lord showed me that we had nothing to fear. He had taken what the enemy had planned for our destruction and sunk the plans of the enemy.

It was though the enemy had gone unnoticed, but was active in coming against us. For instance; my grandson had gotten sick with tonsillitis and had to be taken to the doctor. Normally I would pray for him right away, believing for God to reveal a healing in him. I realized after talking to my friend and prayer partner that I had failed to do so. Once we prayed for him, he showed no symptoms of sickness in spite of the fact that my daughter had the doctor put him on an antibiotic. Then I had been healed of Diverticulitis and the symptoms came back on me, far worse than anything I had experienced while being hospitalized a few months back, before my healing had been manifested. I began to come against the symptoms that were so strong that I had to use the Lamaze breathing techniques to get my mind off the focus of the pain. Three days I suffered with those pains, but I would not take anything less than an absence of the symptoms I was experiencing. Nothing came of those pains, praise the Lord! I had also battled the fear of knowing that it could be scar tissue closing off my bowel and that shortly I would be without insurance.

Knowing this I would have to depend completely on the Lord for the manifestation of my healing, not only for the diverticulitis but also for the scar tissue. It didn't matter to me; I was willing to do what it took for the Lord to have victory in my body. Every time the pain would come, I would thank God for it. It has been several weeks now and I am completely pain free. It was because I set my face as a flint toward my healing and gave God thanks and praise for it before I was able to see it.

Then I go to a bible study that we were having on Tuesday, and find that one of the ladies of the church has been diagnosed with what appears to be cancer in her kidneys and because she has been doctoring for kidney stones, they were able to find this mass on her kidneys. She is now in the valley of decision and will have to decide whether she will believe the lord for a supernatural healing or whether she will have the surgery and had the doctor take the upper part of her kidney and part of her rib, to extract the mass that they feel is cancer. God can heal her either way; she will decide which way it will be.

The next thing I know, my prayer partner has a granddaughter who was contemplating suicide. She was not successful, because God protected her from the enemy being able to snuff her out. As a result of this horrible incident, the family is being brought together for the good.

We had just believed God to heal a girl with a brain tumor and she is healing from surgery even as I'm writing this. Now, our church is very small in number and we can't afford this many attacks. There would be no one left if the enemy is successful, just like if that submarine was able to attach a bomb to the bottom of that battle ship and blow it up, leaving no survivors.

We will survive this attack! The Lord is going to sink the undermining of the enemy that is trying to destroy us. Our ship is not going to sink and when it's all over, the Lord will receive all the Glory because we have done nothing or could we, if we tried.

That vision wasn't just for me, but to let the body of believer's that I serve with know that He is in charge of our ship and we are anchored to the Lord Jesus Christ and everything is going to be ok.

The Fruit Inspector

I CAN'T IMAGINE HOW BORING it would be to have to go out into a field of fruit trees every day and check the fruit for impurities. I'm not sure how the job is done, but I would think in order for the crop grower to have a good quality shipment, every piece of fruit would have to be inspected.

I wonder if the type of fruit that's being inspected would make the difference. Would I check a vine of grapes the same way I would check a tree of oranges? I think it would be harder to inspect a vineyard of grapes then a bushel of bananas. With bananas, it would be rather obvious, if they were bad.

I will occasionally bring home a bag of potatoes from the store, and sure enough, every one of them would have a rotten spot in the middle of them. What has happened is, the potatoes have been frozen somewhere along the way. The problem is, when one is frozen, it's more than likely that you will have to throw the whole bag away. It's not real obvious that the potato is bad. You have to cut into the heart of it to see if there is damage.

God talks a lot in his word about fruit. He compares people to fruit. He has little tolerance for trees that bear bad fruit and trees that bear no fruit at all. Matt. 3:10 says "And even now the ax is laid to the root of the trees. Therefore every tree which does not bear good fruit is cut down and thrown into the fire." This passage is not talking about literal trees, it's talking about people. Those people that do not bear good fruit for the kingdom must be destroyed.

Matthew 7:15-20 says, "beware of false prophets, who come to you in sheep's clothing, but inwardly they are ravenous wolves. You will know them by their fruits. Do men gather grapes from thorn bushes or figs from thistles? Even so, every good tree bears good fruit, but the bad tree bears bad fruit. A good tree cannot bear bad fruit, nor can a bad tree bear good fruit. Every tree that does not bear good fruit is cut down and thrown into the fire. Therefore by their fruit you will know them."

Those statements are pretty harsh. So I wonder what qualifies as bad fruit. I would venture to say that it would be the lifestyle, or character of the tree. One of the problems with trees that bear bad fruit is that the tree will influence others if not dealt with.

Satan was a bad tree. He influenced Eve to eat of the tree of knowledge of good and evil and look at what the outcome was. The whole world was affected. Satan was like one of those potatoes. From the outside he was perfect. But the inside had become rotten. In Ezekiel 28:12b-15 says,

"You (Lucifer) were the seal of perfection, Full of wisdom and perfect in beauty. You were in Eden, the garden of God; Every precious stone was your covering; The sardius, topaz, and diamond, Beryl, onyx, and jasper, Sapphire, turquoise, and emerald with gold. The workmanship of your timbrels and pipes was prepared for you on the day you were created. You were the anointed cherub who covers; I established you; You were on the holy mountain of God; You walked back and forth in the midst of fiery stones. You were perfect in your ways from the day you were created, till iniquity was found in you."

I believe that the Lord had to cut to the heart of the matter when it came to seeing the evil that was found in Lucifer. Pride was found in him and it was his downfall. In Isaiah 14:12-15 says: "How have you fallen from heaven, O Lucifer, son of the morning! How are cut down to the ground, You who weakened the nations! For you have said in your heart; I will ascend into heaven, I will exalt my throne above the stars of God; I will also sit on the mount of the congregation on the farthest sides of the north; I will ascend above the heights of the clouds I will be like the Most High, Yet you shall be brought down to Sheol, To the lowest depths of the Pit."

Lucifer means "Light Bearer" can you imagine how when the light hit him what it must of looked like. When there is that many jewels brought together and the light is shone on them it must look like a prism. I would think that it would be hard to look at him without a pair of sun glasses on.

The beauty he must have possessed would have been breath taking. If there were any kind of reflection that he was able to look in, he would have had to want to stare at himself constantly. When God creates anything it is beautiful, so I think he was just brilliant.

I can't imagine going up against your creator wanting to take His place, but that's exactly what he did and actually thought he would get away with it. What possessed him to think that he would actually be able to pull it off? He was greatly deceived. The ironic thing about it is; he is still out there thinking that he still has a chance. If he can, he will take as many people with him as he can when he goes down to the Pit.

Often people start out good and somewhere down the line something enters them and they fall just like Satan. I see that it is very possible for that to happen with us, but Lucifer was in good company on a regular basis. Where did the bad come from? I guess this explains why Jesus, when He ascended into the Holy of Holies in heaven had to apply the blood to the mercy seat. Heaven had been corrupted and the blood would have had to be applied their first.

So what does God want to see when He inspects us for fruit? Gal.5:22 say's, "But the fruit of the Spirit is love, joy, peace, longsuffering, kindness, goodness, self-control. Against such there is no law." It doesn't take long to know if someone is walking in these traits. If we walk in these things we will not have to worry about having the ax laid at our roots.

The Pyramid

I HAVE SHARED A LOT of visions in this book and I really am concerned about this one. It was just a flash, lasting a minute or so. I saw total darkness and then all of a sudden, I saw a pyramid that resembled the one on our money, only this one didn't have the eye, it had a whole face. It was glowing kind of like when iron is in fire. So I saw total darkness then this pyramid that begins to glow out of the darkness, then everything went dark.

The size was monumental. It was very deep, and I saw it as a 3-D type. Immediately I felt as though it had something to do with the economy, not just the U.S. economy, but a worldwide economy and it also had something to do with religion. Not just the religion of the U.S. but also worldwide.

I think about this vision all the time. There has been talk between a Christian friend and I about the religion of paganism, maybe being the religious part of it. I've done some studies that have made me crazy to think about how we have incorporated pagan religion into our society so strong that if anything is said about it, people really get on the defensive.

For instance the matter came up about Christmas and Easter and the worship of Asherah, the mother-goddess of the philistines. She is described in the bible in 1 Kings 18:19 as well as other places in the word. I'm not sure what I think about all this because it's all new to me and I really want to know so I don't offend my heavenly Father.

When I went on line to look this mother-goddess up, I found a lot of information about the wreath being the womb, the Christmas tree, being the asherah pole, the Christmas balls that are hung on the tree being male's testicles. I have to say that I'm so bummed. This has really ruined Christmas for me. I love Christmas and have always celebrated it with all its glitter and sparkle. To me, the Tree represented eternal life, always being green. (Evergreen). The angel on the top of the tree always meant the angels that proclaimed Christ's birth. The presents under the tree represented the gift that Jesus gave us when He went to the cross. I could go on and on. Then I find out that Jesus was probably not even born during that time. It was probably closer to the fall of the year.

I really don't know what to do about this. God knows my heart and He looks at the intention of the heart, but what if all this I learned is true? I don't think that I can just ignore it. That wouldn't serve Him well. I really want the Lord to give me a clear understanding of how He feels about the way we celebrate the Christmas season. If He truly is the "reason for the season" then how can I ignore that fact that He may be appalled at the fact that we participate in paganism.

We have mindsets that cause us to do things sometimes even when we know deep inside that it's the wrong thing to do. When you are raised in a culture that celebrates and participates in all the rituals of worship, you seem to go through the motions just because that's what you've been trained to do. I really must question this situation and ask God to free me of the mindsets that He disapproves of.

What I won't do is judge others for the way they celebrate, I think the Lord will convict if it's necessary. I'm glad I'm not the judge. I do hope that others extent the same courteous to me if I choose not to celebrate the season, if I feel it would in any way offend my Lord then I don't want to do it. If I choose to celebrate the season, and I can do it in good conscience, then I will do so.

Although, when I read Romans 14: 1-5, it says to "receive one who is weak in the faith, but not to disputes over doubtful things. For one believes he may eat all things, but he who is weak eats only vegetables. Let not him who eats despise him who does not eat, and let him who does not eat judge him who eats; for God has received him. Who are you to judge another's servant? To his own master he stands or falls. Indeed, he will be made to stand for God is able to make him stand. One person esteems one day above another; another esteems every day alike, let each by fully convinced in his own mind." God will be the Judge. As for the vision, God will show me the interpretation at the appointed time!

Looking Back

I shook, I sweat, Fear made my heart pound inside my frail chest. I sobbed, wanting so badly to feel calm. I tried to remember the last time I attempted something like this and was even close to being successful. I tried not to think of the pain. I never thought it would end. I remember wishing they would take off the handcuffs.

My husband laid there. He hadn't slept all night. The chairs he laid on couldn't have been comfortable. I remember thinking, "I hope he doesn't think this is because of him." We hadn't been married but a couple of weeks. I wondered if he knew what a mistake he had made. There had to be another way. I couldn't go on. If things didn't change, I knew I was going to die. "Is it normal to want to die and yet, want to live so badly?" If I had to be driven by the need to constantly have something to depend on, then maybe it would be better to die.

The nurse finally came in and removed the cold metal handcuffs. I was so embarrassed. I heard one of the nurses saying, "She sure is a pretty thing isn't she".

I remember my aunt always use to say, "Pretty is, as pretty does". I wondered what she would have thought if she could have seen me. The last thing the nurse said to me was, "You're lucky to be alive". Funny, I didn't feel lucky.

My husband took me home when I was released from the hospital. He told me how crazy I was. I had taken this two hundred pound man and threw him across the room. It took three of them to get me into the car. I had a supernatural strength that made it very difficult for them to control me. Earlier that day, I had consumed a case of beer and had taken a hand-full of Valium. I passed out. Thank God my cousin's girlfriend was there to care for the kids.

When my husband came home from work, he tried to wake me. He slapped me, trying to get me to wake up. The hand print didn't disappear from my face for a week. You can imagine how hard he had hit me. When I felt the burning pain flood my face, I reacted like the Incredible Hulk. No one had ever hit me like that before. I don't remember what happened after that until we arrived at the hospital. I fought anyone that came near me. My husband begged the staff to bind me, they thankfully obliged.

He told them I had taken diet pills and drank some beer, so they tried to counteract the pills and gave me a shot of some kind of downer. I should have had enough drugs in my system to kill me but God obviously had a different plan. That day was the turning point in my life. My journey, from that point on, has been quite an adventure. For the sake of time, I will spare you the details of the last thirty years.

Everyone has a story. Every addict could write a book. Being a counselor's assistant, I listen to those stories on a daily basis. It constantly reminds me of my past. I'm thankful that I am still alive to talk about it. Not only to talk about it but to listen as others share their stories. I feel that my circumstances would have been in vain, if I would have sat by and let others suffer without trying to help them.

Not everyone has to suffer their entire life if they are an addict. There is a way to avoid the pain and suffering addicts go through. I'm thankful that I have figured out what works for me. I realize that by sharing it with others I may help them to live a happy and prosperous life. For most, it won't be that easy. For me, this common sense answer laid with-in the pages of a very popular book called the Bible.

I tell them to "Intervene at the first thought". Why do I believe this is the answer? If you really want to stay clean and sober, then you will take a good look at your thought process and do something at the first thought of using. Is this easy? No! Is it possible? Yes! If they are willing to use it with everything else that treatment has to offer, they stand a better chance of fighting the addiction. If there is intervention at the first thought, the thought doesn't turn into anything else. The client won't have a chance to think about temptations, or allow the thought processes to become an obsession. If they get to the point of obsession, there is nothing that will come between the client and their drug. This advice has worked for me for the last thirty years. When I get a thought that I know is going to get me in trouble, I deal with that thought until it loses its power and it is put in its rightful place, outside of my mind.

I have put together a workbook that will help Chemical Dependency Counselors deal with this topic and add some fun to the groups on a daily basis. This book is designed to be taught at workshops and in groups to give the clients a visual component to what they are learning.

Treatment can be overwhelming and at times boring, especially compared to the "high" people get from mind altering substances. One of the hardest things that Counselors will face is trying to convince the client to take the time to intervene and do something with the thoughts in their head. When a client thinks about using drugs, the mind can't seem to separate the idea from the feeling. It gets excited at the thought of getting high.

I spent all my using days chasing a high that caused a rush to soar through my body. Every time I think about getting high, I can still feel the burning in my chest from the way alcohol made me feel as it entered my body.

I've never used Heroin. From what I understand, it is the most amazing high. We have nothing to offer the addicts who know that feeling. We do know however, that the addicts don't get to experience that high for very long. Addicts will go places and do things they never thought they would to experience that same high.

Since we can't replace the high with treatment, we at least have to make learning about the damages and the effects of drugs and alcohol interesting. If I can keep their attention long enough and make what they need to learn interesting enough, maybe I can plant a seed in their recovery process.

I know there is hope. I know it's not possible to stay clean. This year I celebrate thirty years of sobriety and I thank God for it.

Phil. 3:12 says, "Not that I have already attained, or am already perfected; but I press on, that I may lay hold of that for which Christ Jesus has also laid hold of me."

Bizzel Rippin Tare

SHE SAID, "YOU MAY WANT to use this in one of your groups. (group material) I know you like to do those kinds of things." She found this excerpt from a child's book. It was funny, and we all needed a laugh. I didn't get around to using it in my groups until after she was gone. She found out that she had cancer.

Too many times clients get clean, only to find out they have been self-medicating a problem, they didn't even know they had. Sometimes it is cancer, sometimes it is hepatitis and sometimes it's too late.

Drugs and alcohol do a job on the liver. The tests are often expensive. They are painful and too many times, very discouraging. Often the clients with liver damage are given a chance to be put on a donor list if they can stay clean for at least a year.

Bizzel Rippen Tare was her name. Not her real name. None of us kept our real names. At least not for the hour of the group we had on Bizzel's behalf. There was a method we used with the alphabet to change our names. Then we would put a twist on it and write about those new identities. We wrote about how we were going to stay clean and sober. We wrote a recovery plan describing what we were going to do as a result of being clean. One by one we read our stories. They gave us hope. Bizzel would be proud of the way we laughed. The atmosphere seemed lighter in the house for the rest of the day. There's not enough laughter in these types of houses. Groups last all day long. With all the energy it takes to stay clean, we can sometimes forget to laugh.

When clients come to our facility, we tell them they have a tool box to fill with the information they will be given. They are to use it when they leave treatment. Hopefully, they will put humor in there and use it when they need a pick me up.

There are many reasons clients laugh here. Sometimes clients have a nervous laugh. They laugh at things that are not funny. They laugh when they get in trouble. They laugh at other people. It's hard to teach a group when a client begins laughing and can't stop. Before you know it the whole group is laughing uncontrollably and they're not sure why they are laughing. This includes me. They apologize as soon as they pull themselves together, just before they look at someone and start laughing again. I let them. If the whole group turns out to be a laughing session, I don't care. It feels good to laugh and I think if a person has some laugh still in them, then they have to let it out or they will explode. The laughter probably does more good than anything we can teach them. When you lighten up and let them laugh, they seem to be better able to open up to you. Besides, what choice do you really have in the matter? The more you try to stop them, the harder they laugh.

The Bible says, "A merry heart doth well like a medicine." (Proverbs 17:22)

The Pitter Patter of Little Feet

THEY LOOK INTO YOUR EYES begging you for help. Sometimes they are small and sometimes not so small. We have those who look small but act big. We have those who look big but act small. Most of the time it's the clients who fit that bill. One child in particular comes to mind. She was ten going on thirty. She was the tail that wagged the dog. She tried to put me in my place a time or two but I've always made it a point to win every argument with children. Especially when I know it's for their good. She wanted her mom to get help. It sounded like she had seen a lot more than she should have ever had to see. I've been there too. You feel embarrassed when you have people looking at you, knowing that you shouldn't be seeing the things you are seeing.

I look in the eyes of these children and feel their pain. I know they just want to have a normal life. There is no normal when you're an addict. There is no normal when you come from a family of addicts. At least not what most people call normal. Addiction is your normal. These children want to feel safe. They want to know what to expect. They push the standards to see if the standards stand. Consistency is their friend. We try to provide that for them. We have sit down community dinners, set bed times and mothers spend time reading to their children. We provide day care for them on a regular basis. They know when they come to the facility they have rules just like mommy and they look forward to being with us.

There's a sad side for some. When a mother goes back out, the child suffers. The brief consistency they had has disappeared and once again, uncertainty prevails. I know how that feels. I used to want to sleep in my clothes. I never knew when my parents were going to come home. I never knew what was going to happen when they did. More times than not, it wasn't good. There was a lot of drinking and fighting going on. I would have loved to be able to come to a safe haven and be a part of so much serenity.

I'm glad we can experience a mother reuniting with her child in a sober environment and bring joy to those little feet. It may only last a little while, but the kids will never forget.

In Matt. 19: 14 Jesus says, "Let the little children come to me, and do not forbid them; for such is the kingdom of heaven." This is their hope!

The Rooms

I FIRST HEARD THE TERM "The Rooms" when I began working at our facility. It is a way to explain the places our clients go to share their stories. The rooms are found at churches all over the country. People come together and talk about the problems they have as addicts and alcoholics.

When I first started working as a Chemical Dependency Tech, I would drive the clients to a meeting and go inside and listen to the stories. It was amazing to hear so many things that people have in common when it comes to the lives they were forced to live as children and how the different ways they acted as addicts related to my own story.

There is such a common bond in those rooms. I hear clients tell me that these rooms are the only place they feel comfortable. I'm glad they feel good going to those places because we make them attend ninety meetings in ninety days. By the time a client leaves our facility they should have enough courage to attend those meetings on their own.

The AA community knows how to have fun. They have dances and picnics, activities and 50/50 drawings. It's where clients find sponsors to work with them in recovery. Some sponsors are better than others. Every once in a while you find one that goes the extra mile. They come and pick up the clients and take them to meetings or out for coffee. Some come and work the steps with them. It's a beautiful thing.

I love to see the girls hook up with someone that takes a special interest in them. There was one I remember that would come and just hang out. She had been a client here and felt a special bond with the girls that live at the facility.

She would hug the corner of the office wall and be so thankful for having this place to come to. She stayed for almost a year and had many stays with us. She was one that always attended the meetings and would encourage the clients to go to them too.

We finally said she had been given all we could give her and like a baby bird kicked from the nest, we pushed her to the edge of her comfort zone and made her fly. She soared like an eagle and flew above her circumstances and to this day has two years in recovery.

We love to see her walk through the doors. Sometimes, she sends us cards to thank us for our help. These cards aren't just thank you cards, they are pieces of art that match her personality.

We know she goes the extra mile to remind us there are those who can make it even if it's not on the first try. Sometimes she will come and we will have deep conversations about things that make both of us think about recovery in a way that blows our minds. She reminds me that not everyone that comes in our house fails. She is why we have these types of facilities. She is the poster child for recovery.

Reality Rehab

I've always wanted to write a television sitcom about our rehab. It is unique and I know it would be the funniest show on T.V. The only thing missing now is a camera crew. We have everything. The clients are willing. It would have high ratings.

I wonder who would be the star of the show. Would it be the drama queen? We have one in every group. Maybe it would be the one who came regularly to the office to scream and fall on the floor so she could get her way, she was one I never thought would make it but by the time she finished the program, she had pulled herself together enough to raise the beautiful child she was pregnant with while at our facility.

Maybe it would be the silent one who constantly had to be watched because she was always trying to sneak around and do things she wasn't allowed to do. Or it could be the one who tries to control everyone that walks through the door. They seem to have the hardest time focusing on themselves.

Then there are those who think they are in prison and want to constantly "down the duck." That term is used for those who try to get special favors from the staff by manipulating them into doing things that are against the rules. It usually back fires for the staff and clients who are brave enough to try it.

Let's not forget the Mother Theresa's. The minute they enter the facility they try to convince the staff they should get the mother of the year award. There are also those who try to sabotage. They will blow things completely out of proportion and throw you under the bus every chance they get. They'll treat you like they want to be your best friend and in the very next breath, they will take you down.

The watchmen on the wall would also make the lime light. They are the ones that keep rehab interesting. Every time some little thing happens, you always have an eventful day. We do, however, need to know things like, who is making hooch in the closet up stairs and who is calling their drug dealer to bring drugs to the facility. We also need to know who has brought alcohol in tucked deep in the baby's diaper bag. All of that information is needed. What we don't need, is someone telling us every time someone doesn't do their chores. We have to teach them the fine line between what hurts their recovery and why they're not focusing on theirs.

The one that makes you really think, is the one who doesn't think they are an addict. It causes them great pain to admit they need help. Those are the ones who have usually have an injury or have been the victim of an unexpected surgery and can't stop taking the pain pills long after their injury has healed. They have actually lived a life much different from the crack addict who has prostituted herself to fund her drug habit.

The crack addicts that have sold their bodies are usually the ones with the most gratitude. They have a nice place to live, they get to eat three meals a day and snack whenever they want. When you take them shopping, they're not sure how to act because they are used to going into a store and their only means of shopping is the "five finger discount." When Friday recreation group comes, they are the most excited to be able to experience clean and sober fun. I love to watch them and you would too.

There is just something about a grateful heart that makes you want to melt. We have criminals that are addicts, and we have addicts who do criminal acts that fund their addiction. It doesn't take long to figure out who is who. That episode would be one you could really enjoy.

I don't want to forget the clients that have dual diagnosis. Some suck the life out of you. You would want to watch this drama just before going to bed so you could get a good night's sleep. They talk to you non-stop or they talk to the voices in their heads. You wonder if those voices ever tell them to kill you. This would be the episode called The Murder Mystery.

The ones with Bi-polar are interesting. They love to bounce around and stay up for days. If they are fortunate enough to be on their medications before coming to the facility, then the midnight shift program would be pretty boring. If the clients come unmediated as they often do, midnight shift could be the most interesting episode of the season.

I have great memories of night shift, one particular night stands out in my mind. One of the clients threatened to put the night shift girl in the basement where other staff would find her dead in the morning. (This one could be labeled the CSI episode, her stay was very short.)

Sometimes clients will come to the facility and bring their drugs with them. These are not street drugs, although, they have some street value. We have stopped those drugs from being allowed in. We have boxes that the clients have to put their medications in while they are in our treatment center. The boxes are the size of small bread boxes. At times, those boxes are over flowing with the medications the clients are on when they arrive. (Sorry, we can't air that episode for you. Distributing the meds would actually take longer than the program allows.)

I think the most outstanding program, would have to be the one where we do the room searches, clients are so creative. They somehow smuggle all sorts of things into their rooms when staff isn't looking. We find TV's, radios, tanning lights, food, drinks, unmentionables, drugs, alcohol, and cell phones. The list goes on and on. It makes you wonder where the staff goes wrong.

It just wouldn't be right to let the clients have all the glory. There is another side to the madness. We have a wonderful staff. I would venture to say that we have the funniest staff around. We are far from perfect. In my opinion, it would make a great comedy.

Some of our staff members are a little wild behind the wheel of our van (aka, the druggy buggy). If only our poor van could talk. We have had mirrors knocked off. There is a dent that stretches the length of the van doors. The windshield is so cracked that we have actually stopped driving it for fear that it will finally cave in and kill someone. I'm surprised that we have not run into a roadside traffic inspection, but I think we could set up a mock one just for the viewers.

I have to admit that we are no respecters of persons when we hire individuals to work at our facility. Let's face it, not everyone can appreciate what we do for a living. There have been those unsuspecting souls that have no idea what we do on a daily basis. They last one day and realize they must get out while they can. If you could see the look on their faces, you'd see what they are thinking. Help me!

There are those who, like me, are determined to be sacrificed for the greater cause. I know both sides and I want to be remembered for going out on the sober side of things. Something in me wants to believe that I can make a difference.

Every once in a while we hire those who are the enablers. They want to be the client's friend. This can get complicated. I have even been told that we have counselors that get so bored with the clients they have fallen asleep during their sessions. I just want to say we know who you are. (They would be the ones we want to star in our office version of the show.)

I could not let this opportunity go by without sharing about our case manager who took a client to an appointment and decided to take it upon herself to park in a no parking zone. When she returned, the rehab car had been towed to an unknown location. I had to rescue her and a very upset client that night. Two of our star employees had to go back to the location after finding the car and pay to have the car released. The bill, when all was said and done, was more than the car was worth. We no longer have that car or the case manager. It just doesn't get better than that when you're watching our show.

I have seen Program Directors come and go. Not all have been as interesting as others. One I can remember was actually sicker than our clients. She used our clients for her own benefit because of her need for power. She was a train wreck and sorry to say, she is still out there somewhere. That's a scary thought. (this would make for an interesting program). Someone said she would come to our facility and park across the street and watch our building. That just seems a little unstable to me. Is it true? I don't know. I would throw it in just to make it exciting.

Drug screens are a very important part of our treatment. We have people in our facility who take their job very seriously. They do everything short of cavity searches to make sure our clients are on the up and up during a urine screen. (This segment would have to be one with a warning that the children would need to leave the room because it would be rated R.)

We have a client who calls in everyday to get the color of the day to see if she has to be screened. She wants to thank us for our creativity in choosing the colors to keep it from being boring. She desires to be a sapphire one day. We could call that segment, Call waiting).

D.I.P. stands for our Driving Intervention Program. I haven't been blessed to have actually participated in that part of our work. I know a girl who has and she lasted only a very short time. She quickly figured out that it was not for her. I don't know for sure, but I'm thinking that can't be good. Well, actually it would be great for the show. (Now remember, I did say we aren't perfect.)

We have a Christmas party every year. If that's what you would like to call it. We get to bring our own food, bring our own gift and you don't have to play the guessing game to figure out what we will be doing because it is the same thing year after year after year. But we do get to clean up the mess when we are done. That parts different. The new hires, are the ones who usually clean up.

Let's see, have I forgot anything? Oh yes, the sad reality of the pay. You don't work at our facility for the pay. It is a profession of help. God knows I need some. When the segment of our show about the pay comes on, you will be laughing so hard you'll be crying. I know I do, well, the crying part anyway.

Ok, I know all this sounds bad but it is reality. To not give you the whole truth just wouldn't be right. We have extremely gifted counselors, program directors, certified people, CDT's and part timers who come to work every day and give all they have for the clients that live at our facility. Let's face it. That would make for a boring reality show.

I think I can say, in all honesty, that we are blessed to be balanced. When a client leaves our facility, they are given a survey to get their opinion of their stay. I would venture to say that most of the clients have very positive things to say about their experience here. That also would make a great show. All in all, we are greatly loved. Everyone in this life needs to laugh. Again, "A merry heart doth well like a medicine!" Proverbs 17:22

Toothaches, Candy Bars, and Bulimia: An Odd Combination

EVERYONE AT SOME POINT HAS had a bad tooth ache. I know that whatever I place in my mouth is going to give me trouble and I still put it in my mouth. I have traded one addiction for another constantly in my life.

If alcohol and crack is not an option, sugar and caffeine are. They actually have a lot in common. I can see why those two drugs are substitutes for the others. I tell our clients, if they don't stop using drugs, they are going to die. Do you think that stops them? NO! It makes no difference to an addict. They already know they are going to die. They will be the first to tell you it doesn't matter.

It works the same way with your teeth. The pain can be unbearable and I will still stick a candy bar in my mouth knowing how bad it is going to hurt. Now I will say that after the candy bar fix, I will seek something out for the pain. Addicts do the same thing with drugs. They use. They know the pain is coming. The heart will fail. Sometimes it's the liver or maybe it will be the kidneys.

Now I look for something to fix the pain so I take more drugs. Now I'm taking drugs for a different reason. It is a vicious cycle.

We have women in our treatment center who experience a different kind of pain. They deal with eating disorders. They are the ones who eat the candy bar then throw it up so they don't gain weight. As if it wasn't bad enough, what teeth the sugar doesn't rotten, the acid from the stomach does.

There is a fear that someone will one day come into the facility and throw up what they have eaten and rupture their esophagus. They care nothing about whether they die from their disorder, the drugs, or a rupture. Let them put on a pound or two and they can't stand it. Go figure.

Maybe it all goes together, all the dysfunction all wrapped up. I think people are examining me constantly. Analyzing everything I do. Even if I don't have anything under control I need to look like I do. I want to eat. I like to eat. Eating gives me a level of comfort I can't find in anything else.

The thoughts of "why did I eat that" follow quickly. "I can't eat that. I have to get rid of it. If I put on any more weight someone will see it and I will look like I don't have control". Sometimes it's because the eating disorder is the only thing I have control over, but not in a good way. It's not until the last hour that people come in and take control of the eating. It's usually by an intervention where someone puts you in the hospital and forces you to eat. It's just another addiction.

Before I got saved, This was me. My stomach was growing up through my esophagus, my hair was falling out and I was on my way out. The doctor told me it I didn't stop what I was doing that he would have to do balloon surgery to stretch the opening to my stomach.

I finally turned it over to the Lord and I began to get healthy. If I would have continued, I would have died.

3 John: 2 says, "Beloved, I pray that you be in health and prosper in all things and be in health, just as your souls prosper."

Gems

It wouldn't be fair to write this book and not mention the gems that we as staff find in recovery. Coal, under enough pressure, produces diamonds.

Every once in a while we find a gem. When they arrive, they are in the earth of addiction. They are rough, dark, covered in discouragement. The pressure of recovery is applied. The process of the lapidary takes place and the dirt is cut away. The pain begins. They are polished and they begin to shine. They have light bulb moments. Who gets the credit? Their Higher Power deserves and gets the credit at least by this staff. Without Him, they won't shine. They can't shine.

How do they shine? By managing their addiction and paying it forward. Many go back to school to become drug and alcohol counselors. Some are talking about opening their own rehabilitation centers. Some just want to work in one.

I remember the day I went back to school. I was finally going somewhere. I would show those who thought I would never make anything of myself. At first, I guess that was the plan but then I began to see how much I could help people. I realized that when I was finished, I was going to have a job that meant something. It wasn't just going to be a job. It was so much more.

The day I started my career, I fit right in. I felt such a sense of belonging. I had once walked where they had walked. I wasn't just someone who would be trying to understand where they were coming from. I too had been put under the pressure. I too had visited the lapidary. I too had been cut and polished by my Higher Power and now He would shine through me. I too was a gem.

1 Peter 2:5 says " You also, as living stones are being built up a spiritual house, a holy priesthood, to offer up spiritual sacrifices acceptable to God through Jesus Christ".

Lessons Learned

I REMEMBER IT LIKE IT was yesterday. I boldly stated, "I'm taking the client's to the funeral home for Rec"! I want them to see the process of death from the time the body is brought in, until they're ready for viewing. I wish you could have seen the look on my co-worker's face. She was too nice to tell me that she knew this was not a good idea. Especially for a group labeled "recreation". Before the day was over, the boss had to let me down gently. She knew I meant well, but it wasn't going to happen. It seemed like a good idea at the time.

When I look back now, I can really see what a problem it could have been for some of my clients. It's good to know that I have grown. Thank God there are people around me that have years and years of experience and know what's best for the clients. Unknowingly, I could have done damage.

I'm very driven to have fun. I like to do things that are unusual. I am the, "spur of the moment" kind of person who "throws caution to the wind" and just goes for it. I am the person who says, "Watch this" and then does something really stupid and hurts herself.

One day I decided to take a group of clients to the mall for a group outing. I blindfolded them while they took turns leading each other around the mall. I placed clothes pins in different areas of the mall with messages on them. I wanted to see if we could remember where we had left the pins in our blind state. I wanted to see if anyone at the mall would stop and read those messages.

We were having a great time until someone called mall security and we were escorted to the mall office by two rather strange security officers. They wanted an explanation. The mall manager was very kind. He thought we were a group of college kids doing an experiment. He told us to proceed, but next time, we were to come to the office and let them know our intentions.

I should have thought to do that before I set up the group. I realized at that point I really had a lot to learn.

It wasn't fun when the clients went back to the staff and reported that I had put plastic bags over their heads and had embarrassed them in front of the entire mall. Not once did they give me a clue of their embarrassment. I truly thought they were having the time of their lives. The plastic bags were folded and tied around their heads not over their heads. I learned that clients have a tendency to blow things out of proportion.

I learned a lesson that day. The next time I take clients to the mall, it will be to go shopping. My boss suggested that I might think twice before pulling that stunt again. I agreed.

Psalms 107:1 says, "Oh give thanks to the Lord, for He is good! For His mercy endures forever".

Droppin' a Dirty

I CAN ONLY WONDER WHAT you think that means! Well if you're a client in treatment, you definitely know what it means. Clients are so creative. They sometimes go to extremes to not have drugs show up in their system.

There are kits you can buy at the local pharmacy to flush out your system, but there is just one problem. It takes everything else in your system, too. Creatine levels drop quickly when you flush out your system. If one of our clients comes back from a pass and their creatine levels are under twenty, we know they have flushed out their systems.

We have had clients tape IV bags to their back and run a line to their private area and when they were screened, use someone else's pee so they won't get caught. (Sorry, didn't work). Then there are those who have others pee in a urine cup and try to switch them out when a staff member doesn't want to get up-close and personal. That one worked for a minute, until they pat themselves on the back and share that information with their peers. The ones they tell usually can't keep a secret so they tell a member of the staff. Especially if they want to get the focus off of them and onto the one who is trying to pass a dirty.

Sometimes we get those who don't put the lid on tight and the screen leaks in transit. That one only works once. We have learned what to do to keep that from happening.

Clients are very smart when it comes to drug screens. They pass the word around when they find out exactly what it is we screen for. Drug Court clients are pros at this.

One time, a girl completed treatment and was going to be on a color code. She was going to have to call in daily to see if her color was chosen. If it was, she would then have to drive to the main office to screen for us. She drank that night and thought since she just left treatment, we wouldn't call her color that soon. Since she didn't call, we figured she had relapsed and called her in to look at an apartment. (She was in our transitional housing program.) Imagine the look on her face when she was asked to give us a screen. She knew there was no way she was going to pull one over on us. She came clean with the truth and admitted to using. We may not catch them all, but we catch some.

There are those that refuse to admit they have dirty urine even when the screen is right in front of their eyes. They try their best to convince you they haven't used. Some would rather go sit in jail, and then admit what they have done. One girl wanted to go to the emergency room and get tested for a yeast infection, even though she had no signs of one. She thought it would prove that the infection was the mystery of how alcohol had gotten into her system. The hard part was convincing her that regardless of whether or not she now had a yeast infection, it wouldn't help her prove she had an infection two weeks before when the screen was actually taken.

Numbers 32:23 says, "Be sure your sin will find you out."

Passing Gas

OK, CAN WE ALL ADMIT right now that it's something we all do? Why is it though that it's such a laughing matter? Clients get a big kick out of passing gas. It doesn't seem to matter where they are, they can't seem to get a grip. I have managed after years, to at least get them to excuse themselves when they do it. (That is when you can get them to admit they did it.) The worst part is when I'm taking them somewhere in the van. There is nowhere to excuse to.

Laughing over someone passing gas is a childish thing to do. When women come into the facility, it seems they are often very immature. I've been told if a client starts using at a very young age, they stop growing emotionally. You can usually tell if they have started using really early in their life by the way they act. For example, lights get left on when clients leave the room. Doors get left open. They complain and tattle tale on each other and try to get their peers in trouble for the most ridiculous things. We have to try to retrain their brains to get them to grow up.

We teach a lot of life application skills to our clients in the short time they are with us. We teach them how to clean house. We teach them how to follow a schedule. The clients are up at 7 am, dressed and ready for the day. When they come down stairs, they are ready to eat breakfast. Exercise is the first group of the day. Meditation is the second. They have group nutrition and parenting. They have lunch and then start groups again in the afternoon. We sit together every day for a community dinner and discuss the events of the day, or recovery issues that may come up. Each client is responsible for cooking a meal through the week. They are also assigned chores. They do them on a daily basis. When the clients leave treatment, they know a lot more than when they came in. We set them up for success. Although it's hard sometimes when you've been charged with a felony to get a job, they can even work after they are here for a while.

1 Cor. 14:20 says, "Brethren, do not be children in understanding; however, in malice be babies, but in understanding be mature."

Spiritual Boot-camps

BECAUSE OF A LIFE CHANGE that has occurred for me, I will be changing careers very soon. Actually I am in the process of that change, which has required me to begin my new life which is crossing over my old life.

I can't wait until the end of the year, so that my focus can be 100 percent of my passion. The Spiritual Warfare Boot camps, is just one part of the many things that I will be doing in my ministry. They have proven to be very interesting and I love how the Lord is bringing such clarity to my mind for the things I'm teaching.

I have given a sample at the end of this book of some of the things the Lord has laid on my heart to teach. We travel all over the U.S. teaching these concepts. It is my desire that as much as it is up to me, that we will be able to expose the tactics of our enemy.

I want so badly for others to know what we are up against and how we can be successful to fight the good fight of faith. I enjoy what we do so much that I can see my partner, Karri Haglock and I doing this for quite some time.

Karri is one of those people who has waited on the Lord and not stepped out to settle for less than what God has for her. I know that the Lord will give her the desires of her heart, because she has been faithful.

I know that there is coming a day when not only will she be very busy about the Lord's business, but so will her husband and children, who she believes God for.

I hope you enjoy the outlines and notes from the Boot camps, I know that they have blessed our hearts and we hope to bless others.

"Note's from the
Spiritual Warfare Boot camps"
"Basic Training"

a. Joining the Army of the Lord

Saying yes to Jesus and inviting Him into your heart is the first step. If you have never had a personal relationship with Jesus and you want to, tonight is a good place to start. There will be an altar call at the end of the boot camp and you will have an opportunity to come forth. Your life will no longer be the same. You May have spent your whole life in church, or you may be hearing about God for the first time tonight. It doesn't matter; God will meet you where you are.

John 3:16 says this; For God so loved the world that He gave His only begotten Son that who-so-ever believes in Him shall not Perish but will have everlasting life.

Romans 5:8 says:" But God demonstrates His own love toward us, in that while we were still sinners, Christ died for us."

b. Receiving your armor (Ephesians 6:10-18)

1. The Belt of Truth

This piece of armor is connected to all the other armor that we are given. Without truth how are we able to put any of the other armor on? Jesus is the way the truth and the life. When we walk in the truth, we are walking in Him.

2. The breastplate of righteousness

This piece of armor is only able to be had by us because of who we are in Christ, and who Christ is in us. When Jesus went to the cross, He did so because He was the lamb who was slain from the foundation of the world. The sacrificial lamb had to be a lamb without spot. It had to be perfect; there couldn't be anything wrong with it. Jesus was that spotless lamb. Because He was without sin, He alone had right standing with God. When the veil was rent from the top to the bottom and Jesus was able to go into Heaven and apply the blood to the mercy seat that was over the judgment seat on the ark in Heaven, it was then that we, when we accept what Jesus did for us at the cross, was given the breastplate of righteousness that is truly right standing with the Father. When the Father looks at us He sees only the blood of His Son. This piece of armors allows us access into Heaven. Without this, we don't get through the gates.

c. Shoes of Peace

1. When we give our lives over to the prince of peace, we are able to take each step, knowing that if we feel the peace of God in what we are doing and in the direction we are going, that it's ok to continue on. If we do not feel the peace, we must wait on the Father. Perfect peace has he whose mind is stayed on thee. (**Is. 26:3**) He told the disciples that "He would send the promise of His Father upon them but tarry in Jerusalem until they were endued with power from on high." (**Luke 24:49).**"

d. Helmet of Salvation

This piece of armor comes with a great price. This helmet is the ransom that Jesus gave for us to be able to spend eternity with Him and the Father and the Holy Spirit. His life for ours. Without Jesus going to the cross, we would be prisoners of war forever in hell. I believe this is not a piece of armor that you have to apply daily. When you get saved, you don't have to get ask Jesus into your heart every day.

e. Shield of Faith

Without faith it is impossible to please God. This piece is the weapon that we use to protect ourselves against the onslaught of the enemy. Jesus was crucified at the place of the skull. Where do we fight our biggest battles? In our mind! This piece is able to quench every fiery dart of the enemy. (We are walking dart boards). The shield has the substance to extinguish the fire that those darts have. When we bring every thought captive, (2 Cor. 10: 5) and know by faith that we have the ability to do so in Jesus, we bring the enemy to his knees. He is paralyzed and can do us no harm. The fire is out. Even in death, "Oh death where is your sting, O grave where is your victory." ((1ˢᵗ Cor. 15:5).

f. The Sword

This is a weapon that should be used in unison with the Shield of Faith. Our sword is the Word of God. It is sharper than any two-edged sword able to divide between the soul and the spirit. This weapon, if not used properly, can bring great damage to the Body of Christ. You can use it to bring life or you can use it to bring death. When we speak the word, it does something. The Bible says, that "God's word does not return void, but it accomplishes what it sets out to do." It doesn't just do something but the word says that it **"prospers in the things that He sends it to do." Isaiah 55:11** Speaking the word when we pray is powerful. When we speak the word in the matchless name of Jesus is even more powerful, for there is no name mightier than the name of Jesus. **Praise is the tool used as the Children of Israel went into battle. When three nations came against Jehoshaphat in 2Chron. 20:1-30,** the praise team were instructed to go out first. Any time the Children of Israel went to battle, they sent the praises out first.

Your post: Responsibility

Your responsibility is now not to be a hearer of the word only but you now will need to be a doer of the word. You are no longer your own because you have been brought with a price. (1ˢᵗ. Cor. 6:20) No soldier just signs up for the service and does nothing. No one engaged in warfare entangles himself with the affairs of this life, that he may please Him who enlisted him as a soldier. (2 Tim 2:4).

The War;

I believe we fight a war of words. In Rev. you will find that the Lord returns to do battle with the enemy and a sharp sword come out of His mouth. (Rev 19:15)Jesus battled the devil when He went into the desert 40 days and Jesus told him that man shall not live by bread alone but by every word that proceeds from the mouth of God. (Matt. 4:4) Jesus said to him it is written; He battled and won by the written word which we speak when we are in battle. Think about all the fights you have been in because of words. They can be used to bring life or they can be used to bring death. We must be careful with the words that we speak from our mouth. For we will give an account of every idle word that we speak!

The Ark:

In Numbers 1:1 The Ark was carried into battle because of what it was and what it carried. The Ark carried the Ten Commandments which represented the **Instruction.** The budding rod of Aaron which represented: **Authority.** Manna which represented **provision.**

The results:

We are more than conquers through Jesus Christ our Lord. (Rom. 8:37). When the Children of Israel won the battles that they fought, they were allowed most of the time to collect all of the enemy's belongings. The enemy would take articles of gold and silver and other important things into battle thinking that this would help them win the battle. Gods children always went away wealthier then when they went into battle. (2 Chron. 20:25) Any time we fight the enemy and we win, we come away wealthier then went we first come into battle.

The enemy doesn't really want you, he wants what you possess. If he wants you, he only wants you because you are the Jewels of the Lord. The battle is not personal, because the fight is the Lords. He wants what the Lord possesses and that's us.

Notes from: "The Enemy"

(The settler and manipulator of good)

If we are in a war then it stands to reason that we have an opponent that is warring against us and us against them or it. This enemy doesn't fight fair and we shouldn't suppose that he would.

This enemy that we fight has been an enemy since the Garden of Eden. He has had the audacity to try to come against the very one who took him down once and for all.

1. Ezekiel 28:11b. "You were the seal of perfection, Full of wisdom and perfect in beauty. (Don't think we can't fall, if Lucifer was described this perfect and who is this enemy? It happened to him it can sure happen to us.) You were in Eden the garden of God; Every precious stone was your covering; The sardius, topaz, and diamond, Beryl, onyx, and jasper, Sapphire, turquoise, and emerald with gold. (This is all on the breastplate of the High Priest as well) The workmanship with your timbrel and pipes was prepared for you on the day you were created. You were the anointed cherub who covers. I established you; you were on the holy mountain of God; you walked back and forth in the midst of fiery stones, you were perfect in your ways. (How many of us can ever say that?) From the day you were created, till iniquity was found in you."

Isaiah 14: 12:17: "How are you fallen from heaven, O Lucifer, son of the morning? How are you cut down to the ground, you who weaken the nations? For you have said in your heart I will ascend into heaven, I will exalt my throne above the stars of God,; I will also sit on the mount of the congregation On the farthest sides of the north; I will ascend above

the heights of the clouds, I will be like the Most High. Yet you shall be brought down to Sheol, to the lowest parts of the Pit."

(In wanting what he wanted, he cheated himself out of what was best to settle for what was good,) He had the best!

This is our adversary!

What is his goal? **To manipulate us into settling for what is good, so it will cheat us out of what is best and possibly get us in all kinds of trouble! Even get us kicked out of the place God has provided for us! So the first opportunity he gets, what does he do? Let's see, turn to:**

A. **Genesis 3:1** Says, "Now the serpent was more cunning than any beast of the field which the Lord God had made. And he said to the woman, Has God indeed said, "You shall not eat of every tree of the garden?" verse 2, And the woman said to the serpent, "We may eat the fruit of the trees of the garden; "but of the fruit of the tree which is in the midst of the garden, God has said,

Verse 3:6 says, "You shall not eat I, nor shall you touch it, lest you die." (God didn't say she couldn't touch it!) Verse, "Then the serpent said to the woman, you will not surely die. (**The lie**). "For God knows that in the day that you eat of it your eyes will be open and you will be like God! (**The very reason he was kicked out of heaven!) verse 6, So when the woman saw that the tree was <u>good</u>** for food, that it was pleasant to the eyes, and a tree desirable to make one wise, she took of its fruit and ate. She also gave to her husband with he, and he ate.

God had already provided for them what was best! He told them they could eat of the tree of life, which was the best tree in the garden!

What does God do? **He kicks them out of the garden**! (Verse 3:22-24). Just what the enemy wanted. His Knew God, He was familiar with God, He was His right hand man, and he knew what would happen, if he could talk the man and woman into eating the fruit, He also knew that Eve added to what God had said.

B. Then shortly after that you see that Adam and Eve reproduce and have two children, and the harvest of the seed of sin, is apparent. Verse 6, you see that Cain becomes angry at God because "He refuses his offering and God deals with him and tells him **he must master his sin, that it lies at the door, And it's desire is to have you,** but you should rule over it." So Cain settles for what he thinks is good and what happens? He cheats himself out of what's best and he gets kicked to the curb! Out of the presence of the Lord! (Verse 4:14-15) God then replaces able with Seth (who would be the Godly seed that Jesus would end up coming through,) (**Jesus, Gods best for us).**

Then Satan shows up at Job's place. Verse1:6, "Now there was a day when the sons of God came to present themselves before the Lord, and Satan also came among them. And the Lord said to Satan, "From where do you come? (He still has access to the Father). So Satan answered the Lord and said, "From going to and fro on the earth, and from walking back and forth on it. (**And he still does it today folks, don't think he doesn't.**) They continue in their conversation about Job and Satan says to the Lord:

Job 1:11 "Stretch out your hand and touch all that he has, and he will surely curse you to your face."

Job 2:3 "Then the Lord said to Satan, Have you considered my servant Job? That there is none like him on the Earth? A blameless and upright man, one who fears God and shuns evil? And still he holds fast to his integrity, although you incited me against him, to destroy him without cause."

Zech. 3:1 then he showed me Joshua the high priest standing before the Angel of the Lord, and Satan standing at His right hand to oppose him.

The difference in Job and Adam and Eve and Cain, is the Job chose to do the right thing in spite of what it would cost him. He held out for God's best and look what happened! **Job 42:12 Now the Lord blessed the latter days of Job more than his beginning!**

If we wait on the Lord, and hold out for the things that He wants us to have. It will always be for our best. Often it comes when we think it is way too late.

In most of these instances when you see the enemy, he is in the presence of God accusing us to Him. He wants to destroy us.

Luke 4:1 you even see him in the wilderness with Jesus, trying to get Jesus to worship him and to do things that the Father would not want Jesus doing.

When did he come to Jesus? At His weakest moments. After He had not eaten for forty days. **Luke chapter 4. Verse 13:** "Now when the devil had ended every temptation, he departed from Him until an opportune time!"

When will he come to us? In our weakest points. If He did it to Jesus, he will do it to us.

Luke 22:31 says this: "Simon, Simon, indeed, <u>Satan has ask for you, that he may sift you as wheat. Verse 32: But I have prayed for you,</u> that your faith should not fail; and when you have returned to me, strengthen your brethren."

Each time the enemy shows up, he doesn't come empty handed, he will offer us something, and it is usually good. His intentions are always to cheat us out of best!

He knows that if we settle for the worldly things and the things that he wants us to have that we will forget about heaven. Sin feels good or we wouldn't want to do it. Settling for less than what God the Father wants for us can keep us out of heaven. If we sell out to him and settle for what looks good to us, it will cheat us out of **of best**!

If we take matters into our own hands and not wait on the Lord, the same thing happens,

Let's look at **King Saul, (1 Sam.13:8-14) He** refused to wait on Samuel to give the offering before they went into battle. Saul took matters into his own hands and it cost him the kingdom and his relationship with God. He was booted! Booted from a relationship with the Father and booted from the throne.

When Saul waited the seven days and he didn't get an answer, he did what he thought was good, instead of waiting for what is best! It cost him everything. God had fully intended on blessing Saul in establishing him over Israel forever!

Sometimes we take matters into our own hands, our will not wanting to wait on God because we think it's taking too long and maybe God's not going to show up? Do we understand that the enemy of our soul wants to pressure us into things, so we won't wait on the Lord because he knows we so often will sell out for what is good and in the end it will cheat us out of what is best and often get us kicked out of the plans God has for us.

Our Posts, as a soldier of the Lord Jesus Christ is to wait on Him and His direction, and the things that He wants for our lives.

When we don't wait on Him, we settle for far too less, and it ends up not just affecting us, but those that we love and often those we don't even know.

www.ingramcontent.com/pod-product-compliance
Lightning Source LLC
Chambersburg PA
CBHW022253290526
45785CB00015B/755